Annexation Law IN NORTH CAROLINA

VOLUME

2

Voluntary Annexation

David M. Lawrence

SCHOOL *of* GOVERNMENT
The University of North Carolina at Chapel Hill

Institute of Government
School of Government, UNC Chapel Hill

Established in 1931, the Institute of Government provides training, advisory, and research services to public officials and others interested in the operation of state and local government in North Carolina. The Institute and the university's Master of Public Administration Program are the core activities of the School of Government at The University of North Carolina at Chapel Hill.

Each year approximately 14,000 public officials and others attend one or more of the more than 200 classes, seminars, and conferences offered by the Institute. Faculty members annually publish up to fifty books, bulletins, and other reference works related to state and local government. Each day that the General Assembly is in session, the Institute's *Daily Bulletin*, available in print and electronic format, reports on the day's activities for members of the legislature and others who need to follow the course of legislation. An extensive Web site (www.sog.unc.edu) provides access to publications and faculty research, course listings, program and service information, and links to other useful sites related to government.

Operating support for the School of Government's programs and activities comes from many sources, including state appropriations, local government membership dues, private contributions, publication sales, course fees, and service contracts. For more information about the School, the Institute, and the MPA program, visit the Web site or call (919) 966-5381.

Printed in the United States of America

21 20 19 18 17 2 3 4 5 6

ISBN 1-56011-465-9   [2003.16]

Contents

(each chapter is internally paginated)

Introduction

North Carolina has two voluntary annexation procedures. One procedure, set out in G.S. 160A-31, permits the annexation of areas contiguous to, or abutting, the city. Throughout this book, I refer to this procedure as the *contiguous annexation* procedure. The second procedure, set out in G.S. 160A-58 through −58.8, permits cities to annex areas that are not contiguous and that may be as many as three miles away. I refer to this procedure as the *satellite annexation* procedure.

Because the two procedures have much in common, this book considers them together much of the time. When the two procedures differ, as they sometimes do—in particular in the standards a proposed annexation must meet—the book treats them separately.

The book is organized into six chapters. Chapter 1 briefly introduces voluntary annexation. Chapter 2 discusses the meaning of *contiguity* under the contiguous annexation statute. Chapter 3 describes the five standards that condition satellite annexations. Chapter 4 identifies petition requirements applicable to each of the voluntary annexation procedures, especially issues related to what property interests and owners must sign the petition. Chapter 5 discusses the statutory procedures for a voluntary annexation. Finally, Chapter 6 considers the requirements for providing city services to areas that have been voluntarily annexed.

Two attorneys experienced in annexation matters read the entire manuscript—Kim Hibbard of the North Carolina League of Municipalities and my Institute of Government colleague Bill Thornton. Each made a number of helpful suggestions, for which I am grateful. As I was in preparing the first volume of this set on North Carolina annexation law, I am especially indebted to the many local government officials who have asked me questions about annexation and, in doing so, directed me to the issues that arise under these statutes.

David M. Lawrence
William Rand Kenan Jr. Professor of Public Law and Government
September 2003

1

Introduction to Voluntary Annexation

1

Introduction to Voluntary Annexation

Section 1.01. The Nature of Voluntary Annexations

Voluntary annexations are consensual: they result when the owners of one or more parcels of property and a city agree that the city will annex those parcels. The owners evince their consent by petitioning the city to annex their properties. The city council gives the city's consent by adopting an ordinance annexing the property described in the petition.

A property owner might, however, dispute just how consensual or voluntary such an annexation really is. As cities frequently condition the provision of water or sewer service upon annexation, a property owner who desires or needs these services will have no choice but to petition for annexation.[1] He or she might well feel that the annexation is more coercive than consensual. But no property owner ever seeks annexation without expecting to receive some benefit from the city in return— utility service, better police protection or street maintenance, more favorable zoning, the ability to sell beer or wine, or some other advantage. If that point is understood, it's clear that voluntary annexations are in fact always voluntary—in the same way that any negotiated agreement is voluntary. Each party expects to receive something from the agreement, and that expectation outweighs whatever might be given up.

Because voluntary annexation is consensual, the city must be willing to annex, just as the property owner must be willing to petition. If a city is not interested in annexing property included in an annexation petition, the council has no obligation to proceed with the proposed annexation.[2] Indeed, if the city council has no interest in a particular

---

1. A city's authority to condition utility service upon annexation is discussed in Volume 1 of this series, sections 4.03 through 4.05.

2. *E.g.*, Dugger v. City of Sante Fe, 834 P.2d 424 (N.M. Ct. App. 1992) (Decision of city whether to annex is legislative and not quasi-judicial, even if the city has adopted annexation policies; therefore court cannot force city to annex property meeting city's

annexation proposal, it need not respond to the petition at all; that is, it need not direct the clerk to investigate or certify the petition, and it need not call or hold a public hearing on the proposed annexation.

Section 1.02. Are Voluntary Annexations Constitutional?

In 1969 the U.S. Supreme Court decided two cases involving whether a city may limit the right to vote in general local government elections to property owners. In *Kramer v. Union Free School District No. 15*,[3] the court invalidated a New York scheme that limited the franchise in school board elections to persons who owned or leased taxable property or were parents of schoolchildren. The court applied strict scrutiny to the voting arrangements and concluded that they violated the equal protection rights of persons like the plaintiff, a bachelor who lived with his parents. The court then relied on *Kramer* to decide *Cipriano v. City of Houma*,[4] in which it invalidated a Louisiana scheme that limited to property owners the right to vote in municipal bond referendums.

The outcome in these two cases created concern about whether they might affect the constitutionality of voluntary annexation procedures of states like North Carolina, where only the owners of real property may initiate an annexation. Residents of an annexation area who do not own real property—such as apartment or mobile home renters—have no formal role in the annexation proceeding. But is the petition procedure sufficiently akin to voting to require application of the rule enunciated in *Kramer* and *Cipriano*?

Although not all courts have agreed,[5] the clear rule in the Fourth Circuit, and perhaps throughout the United States, is that the *Kramer–Cipriano* rule has no effect on petition annexation procedures like North Carolina's.

---

policy requirements.); Braunagel v. City of Devils Lake, 629 N.W.2d 567 (N.D. 2001) (Because annexation is a legislative act, disappointed petitioner may not bring action challenging wisdom of city's decision not to annex.). *See also* City of Tucson v. Garrett, 267 P.2d 717, 719 (Ariz. 1954) ("When a requisite petition has been filed, without doubt the statute gives the City Commission the entire discretion as to whether the request therein shall be granted. The petitioners are mere suppliants and have no legal rights to require annexation under any condition.").

   3. 395 U.S. 621 (1969).

   4. 395 U.S. 701 (1969).

   5. *See* Hussey v. City of Portland, 64 F.3d 1260 (9th Cir. 1995).

In *Berry v. Bourne*,[6] the plaintiff was one of thirteen registered voters in an area for which property owners had petitioned for annexation to North Charleston, South Carolina. Under the South Carolina annexation statute, an annexation could be initiated by petition from 75 percent or more of the owners of real property in the proposed annexation area; there was neither a petition role for persons not owning real property nor any opportunity to hold a referendum on the annexation. The plaintiff (who was not a property owner) sought to enjoin the annexation on the ground that this annexation system violated his rights to equal protection as a voter. The Fourth Circuit Court of Appeals upheld South Carolina's petition annexation system. The court argued that the annexation procedure involved no election and that the city's governing board, and not the petitioning property owners, made the decision on annexation.[7] Therefore the *Kramer–Cipriano* rule had no application to the South Carolina annexation system—a system sufficiently comparable to North Carolina's for *Berry* to confirm, at least within the Fourth Circuit, the constitutionality of voluntary annexation in North Carolina.

The case of *Goodyear Farms v. City of Avondale*[8] may establish that constitutionality on a national basis. It involved a challenge to Arizona's annexation procedure, which was very much like South Carolina's except that an Arizona annexation was initiated by a petition from the owners of a majority of the acreage in the proposed annexation area. Once the petition was before the city council, that body had complete discretion about whether to annex, and the statute provided no opportunity for any sort of referendum. Relying on *Berry*, the Arizona supreme court held that the procedure did not involve voting and therefore was not an equal protection violation. The case was then appealed to the U.S. Supreme Court, which dismissed the appeal for

6. 588 F.2d 422 (4th Cir. 1978).

7. "We emphasize again that neither freeholders nor electors as such are given the right to vote on annexation under the statute in question; that right is given exclusively to the governing board of the annexing city. It is true that three-fourths of the freeholders in the area to be annexed must request annexation before the governing body of the annexing city may consider annexation. This is a common prerequisite for authorization of an annexation, whether by an election or by action of the annexing city's governing board. But the important fact is that the action of the freeholders in signing the request for annexation does not authorize annexation. Annexation depends wholly on the favorable vote of the governing body of the annexing city. This is the crucial action and on that neither freeholders nor electors as such have a vote." *Id.* at 424.

8. 714 P.2d 386 (Ariz. 1986).

want of a substantial federal question. Under federal law, such a dismissal is a decision on the merits.[9]

Section 1.03. Challenges to Voluntary Annexations

This book's detailed discussion of the various issues that might arise in a voluntary annexation is intended to assure a city that it is complying with the appropriate statute. It is worth remembering, however, that it is very difficult to challenge a voluntary annexation in court. Chapter 7 of Volume 1 of this series discusses in detail the question of who has standing to challenge an annexation. It concludes that—realistically—there are only three possible plaintiffs with the standing to challenge a voluntary annexation: (1) the State of North Carolina through a quo warranto action; (2) an owner of property in the annexation area; and (3) another city that is simultaneously attempting to annex some or all of the voluntary annexation area. Of these, by far the most likely plaintiff is a second city, but the great majority of voluntary annexations do not create intercity conflicts. The reality, then, is that even if a city makes an error in a voluntary annexation, or stretches the terms of the statute beyond their breaking point, no person or entity will be able to challenge the annexation in court.

9. *E.g.,* Hopfmann v. Connolly, 471 U.S. 459 (1985).

2

Standards for Contiguous Annexations

Standards for Contiguous Annexations

Section 2.01. Introduction

The first of the state's two voluntary annexation procedures permits annexation of tracts contiguous to the city. This chapter considers what makes a property contiguous, and therefore eligible for this form of annexation. Section 160A-31(f) of the North Carolina General Statutes (hereinafter G.S.) defines *contiguous property* as follows:

> For purposes of this section, an area shall be deemed "contiguous" if, at the time the petition is submitted, such area either abuts directly on the municipal boundary or is separated from the municipal boundary by a street or street right-of-way, a creek or river, or the right-of-way of a railroad or other public service corporation, lands owned by the municipality or some other political subdivision, or lands owned by the State of North Carolina.

Section 2.02. Contiguous to *Primary* Corporate Limits

Although the matter has not been specifically addressed by a North Carolina appellate court, it is clear that the contiguous annexation procedure is available only for annexing tracts of land that abut the primary corporate limits of the city. That is, if a city has one or more satellite areas and the owner of a tract that abuts only a satellite seeks annexation, the city must follow the satellite annexation procedure and may not follow the contiguous annexation procedure.

This conclusion is based on the reasoning of the North Carolina supreme court in *Hawks v. Town of Valdese*,[1] in which it held that a city

1. 299 N.C. 1, 261 S.E.2d 90 (1980).

may not undertake an *involuntary* annexation from a satellite area. That reasoning applies to voluntary annexations as well. The town sought to annex involuntarily an area completely bisected by a satellite area the town had annexed some time before; that is, one part of the proposed annexation area lay between the primary corporate limits and the satellite and bordered on both, while the other part lay just beyond the satellite and bordered only on it. (In Figure 2.1, the portion of the annexation area between the existing city and the existing satellite is shown as "A," and the portion beyond the existing satellite is shown as "B.") The supreme court held, first, that these two areas could not be combined with the existing satellite into a single annexation area because the satellite area was already in the city. The court then turned to the issue of whether the city could undertake an involuntary annexation of the part of the annexation area that was at the time contiguous only to the satellite. The involuntary annexation law requires an area being annexed to "be adjacent or contiguous to the municipality's boundaries at the time the annexation proceeding is begun."[2] The issue was therefore whether the phrase "the municipality's boundaries" refers only to the primary corporate boundaries or also includes the city's satellite corporate boundaries.

Basing its conclusion on language in the satellite annexation law, the court held that the area contiguous only to the satellite was not contiguous to the municipality's boundaries. The court pointed out that the satellite annexation statute distinguishes between a city's primary corporate limits and its satellite corporate limits. G.S. 160A-58(2) defines the *primary limits* as those areas set out in the city's charter, as modified by annexations "pursuant to Parts 1, 2, and 3 of this Article"[3] or pursuant to legislative acts. G.S. 160A-58(3) defines *satellite limits* as those areas annexed pursuant to the satellite statute itself. Because involuntary annexations are undertaken pursuant to Parts 2 and 3 of Article 4A, the court interpreted the reference to those parts in the definition of primary corporate limits (but not in the definition of satellite corporate limits) as establishing the rule that the involuntary procedures could be used only to annex territory to the primary limits of a city.[4] Because cities undertake voluntary contiguous annexations pursuant to Part 1 of Article 4A, the court's reasoning just as clearly

---

2. N.C. Gen. Stat. § 160A-36(b)(1) (hereinafter G.S.).
3. The reference is to Article 4A of G.S. 160A.
4. "We hold, therefore, that territory which is contiguous *solely* to the 'satellite corporate limits' fails to satisfy the statutory requirement that the area to be annexed in an involuntary annexation proceeding be contiguous or adjacent to the municipal

Figure 2.1

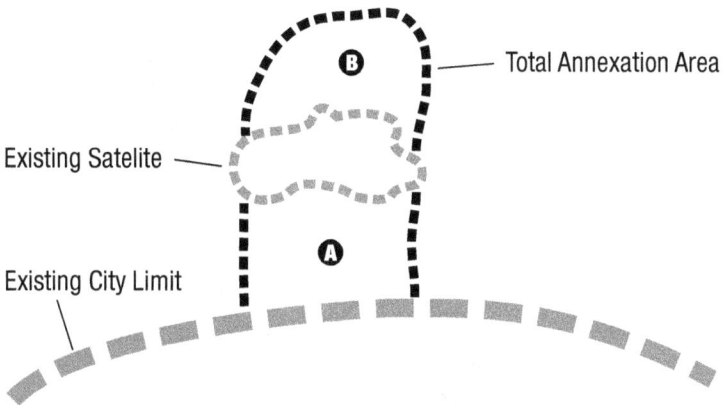

Total Annexation Area

Existing Satelite

Existing City Limit

applies to annexations pursuant to the contiguous annexation procedure; that procedure, too, may be used only to annex territory to the
primary limits of a city.

Section 2.03. Contiguous When Petition Is Presented

G.S. 160A-31(f), set out above, defines *contiguity* in terms of "the time
the petition is submitted" to the city council. This means that if the
contiguity of a particular proposed annexation depends on an earlier
annexation by the city, that earlier annexation must have become
effective no later than the day upon which the new annexation petition
is presented to the city council. The impact of this requirement is
illustrated by the case of *City of Kannapolis v. City of Concord*[5] and
the sequence of events set out below.

1. *September 16, 1987* Concord received a petition seeking
   annexation of land lying between the city and the city-owned
   Lake Concord.

---

boundaries of the city which seeks annexation. Territory contiguous *solely* to 'satellite
corporate limits' is not eligible for annexation until such 'satellite corporate limits'
become 'a part of the primary corporate limits.'" 299 N.C. at 11–12, 261 S.E.2d at 96–97.
    5. 326 N.C. 512, 391 S.E.2d 493 (1990).

2. *September 24, 1987* Concord City Council acknowledged receipt of the petition and called a public hearing on the proposed annexation.

3. *September 24, 1987* Concord City Council adopted a resolution stating its intention to annex the lake. (A city begins a proceeding to annex city-owned contiguous property by adopting a resolution "in lieu of filing a petition."[6])

4. *October 8, 1987* Concord City Council held its public hearing on the petition annexation and, following the hearing, adopted ordinances annexing both the petition property and the lake, effective October 31, 1987.

5. *October 14, 1987* After Concord had adopted its annexation ordinances, but before the annexations become effective, Kannapolis adopted a resolution of intent to involuntarily annex an area that includes Lake Concord.

6. *March 30, 1988* Kannapolis adopted its annexation ordinance.

Once Kannapolis completed its annexation, it brought suit against Concord, arguing that Concord's attempted annexation of the lake was invalid. The supreme court agreed. The city-owned property needed to be contiguous to the city when the council adopted its resolution of intent on September 24, but the intervening annexation that would have made it contiguous had not yet become effective when the resolution was adopted. Indeed it did not become effective until more than a month later. Therefore, the court invalidated Concord's attempted annexation of its own lake and upheld Kannapolis's annexation instead.

If a city receives two separate petitions for voluntary annexation and the validity of one depends on first completing the other, the city can request the petitioners to combine their areas and submit a new, single petition for both areas. Otherwise, the city should delay formal presentation of the second petition until the ordinance annexing the property described in the first petition becomes effective.

Section 2.04. Petitions to Annex More Than One Tract

Many voluntary annexations include only a single tract or lot that is contiguous to the city and raise no questions about contiguity. Other voluntary annexations, however, are composed of several tracts or

6. G.S. 160A-31(g).

lots—not all of which are directly contiguous to the city. Sometimes the question is raised whether such an annexation area still qualifies as contiguous.

The answer is clearly yes. G.S. 160A-31(a) permits voluntary annexation of an *"area* contiguous to [the city's] boundaries" upon submission of a petition signed by the owners of all the property within the area. This statutory phraseology clearly distinguishes between the annexation area and the parcels of property that comprise it. It is the *area* that must be contiguous, not each separate parcel of property within it. (This point is illustrated in Figure 2.2, which shows an annexation area comprised of tracts A, B, C, and D; of the four tracts, only A is directly contiguous to the city.) Although this issue has not arisen in any reported North Carolina litigation, it has come up else-where; the courts in these cases have consistently read contiguity requirements in the way set out above. For example, the Iowa annex-ation statute permits "all of the owners of land in a territory adjoining a city [to] apply in writing to the council of the adjoining city requesting annexation of the territory." In *City of Waukee v. City Development Board*,[7] the Iowa supreme court held that not all parcels within the defined territory needed to adjoin the city but that at least one parcel had to abut the city's corporate boundary directly and begin a chain of contiguity that included all other parcels in the annexation area. The court ruled that "[a]lthough not all of the parcels adjoin or share a common boundary with the city of Clive, all of the parcels are contiguous to each other in the sense that there is no parcel that does not share a boundary with a parcel included in the territory to be annexed."[8]

Section 2.05. Boundaries of the Annexation Area

The two *involuntary* annexation statutes require that the boundaries of the annexation area follow "recorded property lines and streets."[9] Before 1998, these same statutes required the boundaries of involun-tary annexation areas to follow streets or, to the extent practical,

7. 590 N.W.2d 712 (Iowa 1999).
8. Id. at 717. Other cases reaching a comparable conclusion include: City of Leawood v. City of Overland Park, 777 P.2d 830 (Kan. 1989); State *ex rel.* Taylor v. North Kansas City, 228 S.W.2d 762 (Mo. 1950); and Mutz v. Municipal Boundary Comm'n, 688 P.2d 12 (N.M. 1984).
9. G.S. 160A-36(d); 160A-48(e).

Figure 2.2

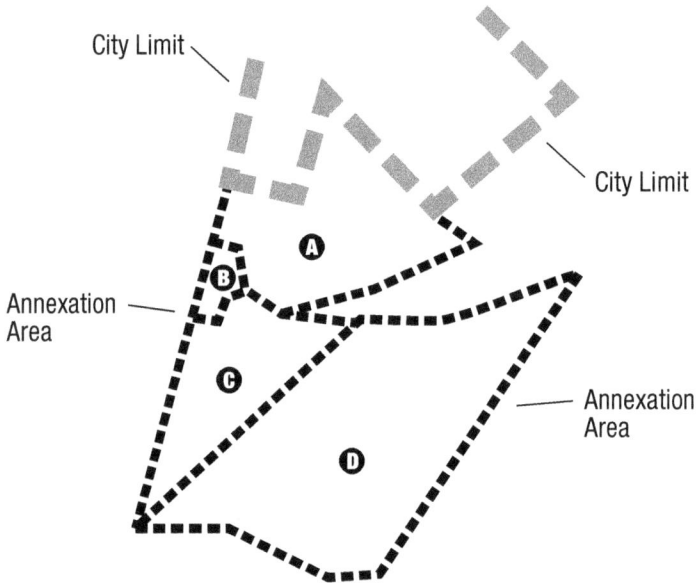

"natural topographic features, such as ridge lines and streams and creeks." None of these involuntary annexation area boundary requirements, however, has ever been applied to voluntary annexations. Therefore, as long as the petitioning property owners and the city agree on the boundaries of a voluntary annexation, there is no statutory bar to splitting tracts, ignoring natural topographic features, or using or not using streets. The boundaries may be wherever they are described to be in the petition and the annexation ordinance.

Section 2.06. How Much Contiguity Is Required?

[a] Introduction

G.S. 160A-31 requires the proposed annexation area to be contiguous to the city. How much contiguity does the statute require? Is a single point enough? Is a strip a few feet wide enough? Must there be a substantial degree of actual connection between the existing city and the proposed annexation area? Or is there some other test? A rich body of case law from other states considers these issues, but none of them have been addressed in a North Carolina appellate case involving a voluntary annexation. Nevertheless, one North Carolina court of appeals decision involving an involuntary annexation suggests that the North Carolina courts might well be receptive to an argument that the contiguous annexation statute requires some substantial degree of contiguity and that a mere point or a narrow strip may not provide enough contiguity.

[b] Points and shoestrings in other states

Two categories of annexations have raised issues about the meaning of contiguity in other states. The first category is comprised of annexations in which contiguity consists of only a single point, as illustrated in Figure 2.3. The second category, so-called shoestring or balloon annexations, typically involve a long strip of land connected to the city only on its narrow side and, usually, connected at the other end to a more regularly shaped parcel of land, as illustrated in Figure 2.4. In a shoestring or balloon annexation, the parcel at the far end is normally the real target sought by the city. How have courts in other states dealt with proposed annexations of these two kinds?

Annexation areas connected only by a single point. The national case law on annexations connected only by a single point is meager and mixed in outcome. In *Village of Plainfield v. American National Bank & Trust Company,*[10] the proposed annexation area was a triangle that touched the annexing city only at one of its three points. The Illinois appellate court held that this point did not create a substantial enough border to constitute real contiguity.[11] On the other hand, in *Louallen v. Miller,*[12] an Arkansas court accepted an annexation area consisting of two parcels. The first adjoined the city boundary for 150 feet and extended west for 634 feet, while the second—a parcel 250 feet by 450 feet—adjoined the first parcel only at a single corner. The court held

---

10. 323 N.E.2d 841 (Ill. Ct. App. 1975).

11. See also Will v. People *ex rel.* Stephens, 81 N.E. 707, 708 (Ill. 1907), in which the court disallowed a proposed town incorporation under a statute requiring the area of a town to consist of contiguous territory. The proposed town was, in fact, a series of strips going in various directions; two of the strips touched only at a single point. Because "no vehicle, and in fact no person, could pass from one strip to the other without passing over or upon lands not within the village," the two strips were not contiguous.

12. 317 S.W.2d 710 (Ark. 1958).

Figure 2.3

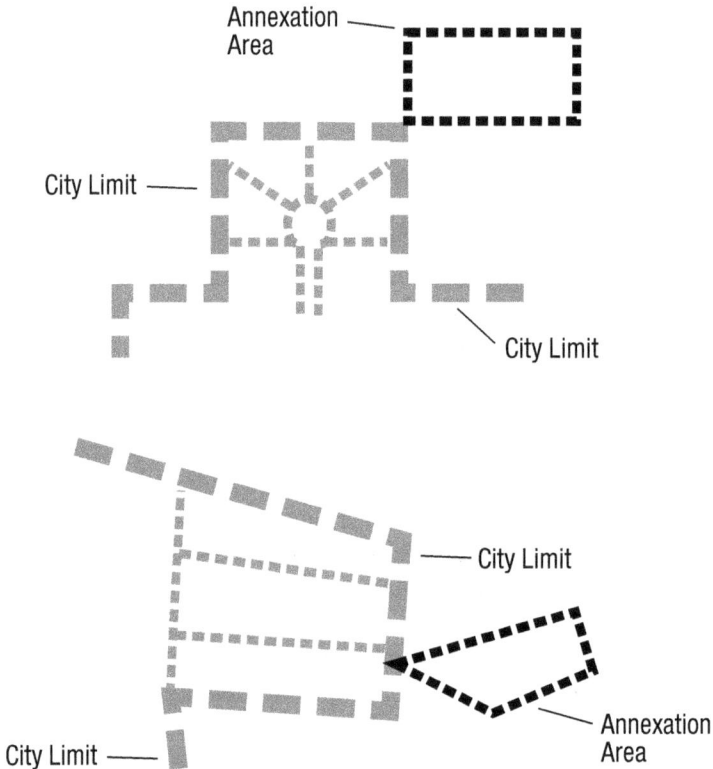

that the two parcels were contiguous to each other and therefore the entire annexation area was contiguous to the city.[13]

Balloon or shoestring annexations. There are many more cases involving annexation areas connected to a city by only a narrow strip of land. The courts in a majority of these cases have held that such

13. See also Independent Consolidated School Dist. No. 66 v. Big Stone County, 67 N.W.2d 903 (Minn. 1954), in which the court considered a statute that permits the transfer of property from one school district to another if it adjoins the receiving district. The property to be transferred in this case shared a common corner, that is, a single point, with the new district; the court held that this satisfied the statutory requirement that the property adjoin the district. *Accord,* State *ex rel.* Badtke v. School Board of Joint Common School Dist. No. 1, 83 N.W.2d 724 (Wis. 1957).

Figure 2.4

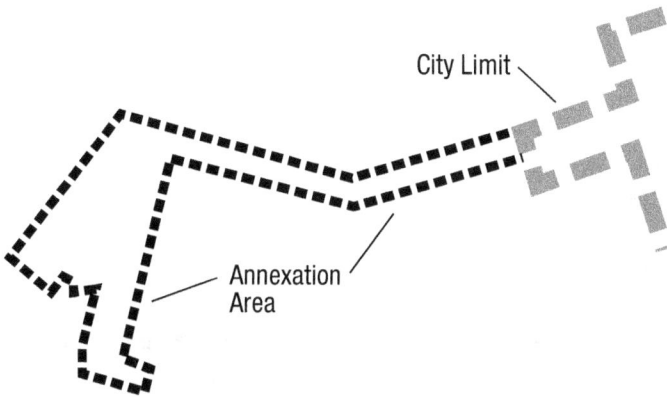

annexation areas *are not* contiguous to the annexing city. Three cases illustrate this body of law. In *Potvin v. Village of Chubbuck*,[14] the city was attempting to annex a balloon attached to the city by a "string" three miles long and five feet wide. The court held that the area being annexed was not contiguous to the city. In *Wescom, Inc. v. Woodbridge Park District*,[15] the district sought to annex a seventy-two-acre tract connected to the district by a 125-foot-wide utility easement that extended for half a mile. Again, the court held that the annexation area was not contiguous to the district. Finally, in *Township of Owosso v. City of Owosso*,[16] the city attempted to annex a 240-acre tract connected to the city by a quarter-mile long strip that in places was as narrow as 282 feet. This court, too, held that the area being annexed was not contiguous to the city.[17]

14. 284 P.2d 414 (Idaho 1955).
15. 364 N.E.2d 721 (Ill. Ct. App. 1977).
16. 189 N.W.2d 421 (Mich. 1971).
17. Other cases reaching similar conclusions include Clark v. Holt, 237 S.W.2d 483 (Ark. 1951) (shoestring 50 feet wide and 3,060 feet long); Ridings v. City of Owensboro, 383 S.W.2d 510 (Ky. 1964) (annexation along highway to reach subdivisions 2,200 feet, 3,600 feet, and 10,000 feet from city); and Wortham Ind. Sch. Dist. v. State *ex rel.* Fairfield Consol. Ind. Sch. Dist., 244 S.W.2d 838 (Tex. Ct. Civ. App. 1951) (shoestring 50 feet wide and more than a mile long).

[c] *Amick v. Town of Stallings*

The two North Carolina involuntary annexation statutes contain two requirements concerning contiguity. First, the annexation area "must be adjacent or contiguous to the municipality's boundaries at the time the annexation proceeding is begun."[18] Second, "at least one eighth of the aggregate external boundaries of the [annexation] area must coincide with the municipal boundary."[19] For many years, municipal officials and their advisers tended to read these two as a single requirement and assumed that if the second requirement was met, the first would be as well. That is, if at least one-eighth of the perimeter of the annexation area directly touched the city boundary, the area was, *ipso facto*, contiguous. In *Amick v. Town of Stallings*,[20] however, the North Carolina court of appeals separated the two requirements and invalidated an annexation that met the second requirement on the ground that it nevertheless did not meet the first.

Stallings's real annexation targets were three subdivisions that lay at some distance south of town. To connect the subdivisions to Stallings, and to meet the one-eighth requirement, the town constructed an annexation area that included the following set of shoestrings:

- First, a strip of land 7,411 feet long and between 50 and 200 feet wide to connect the annexation area to the existing town. This strip ran parallel to the existing boundary for its entire length and was the basis for meeting the one-eighth requirement.
- Second, a strip connecting this first strip to the first subdivision. This strip was about 1,500 feet long and about 150 feet wide.
- Third, a final strip connecting the first subdivision to the other two. This strip was 1,800 feet long and between 165 and 200 feet wide.

The court's reported opinion includes a graphic representation of the annexation area, which is reproduced in Figure 2.5. Property owners in the subdivisions petitioned for judicial review of the annexation, and the court of appeals held that the area was not contiguous to the city and

18. G.S. 160A-36(b)(1); 160A-48(b)(1).
19. G.S. 160A-36(b)(2); 160A-48(b)(2).
20. 95 N.C. App. 64, 382 S.E.2d 221 (1989).

Figure 2.5

Amick v. Town of Stallings [95 N.C. App. 64 (1989)]

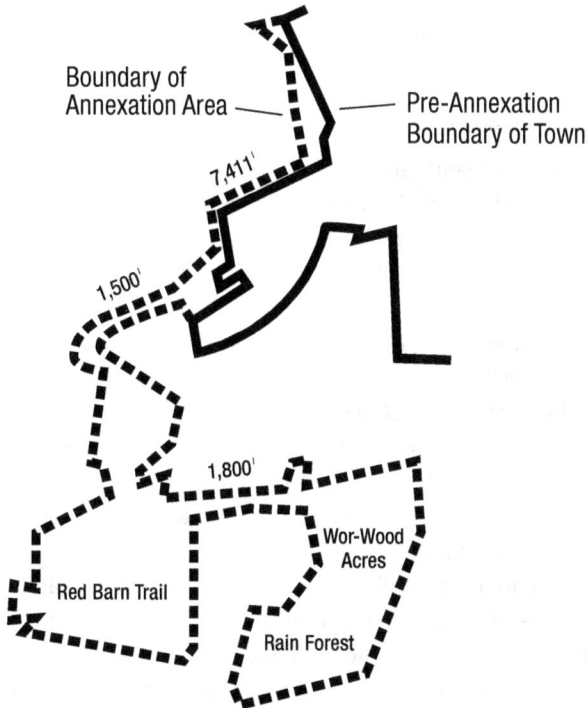

therefore did not meet the first requirement set out above. The court relied heavily on and quoted from *Hawks v. Town of Valdese* (discussed in section 2.02 above). The notion set forth in *Hawks* is that the word *city* connotes a single entity and not a separated mass of distinct areas. The court in *Amick* pointed out that the real targets of the challenged annexation were the three subdivisions, all quite distant from the town, and that they clearly were not contiguous to the town in any sense of the word. The use of the shoestrings to create an artificial contiguity did not persuade the court: "The town's intentional gerrymandering of the annexation boundary creates isolated islands connected to the Town by a single narrow corridor of land; such a 'crazy-quilt' boundary is not consistent with 'sound urban development' of a municipality 'capable of providing essential governmental services to residents within compact borders.'"[21] In reaching its conclusion, the court cited a number of shoestring cases from other states of the sort summarized above in section 2.06[b]. The court clearly thought those cases expressed an appropriate understanding of contiguity.

[d] Some suggestions

If the involuntary annexation attempted in *Amick* was not "adjacent or contiguous to the municipality's boundaries," then a court reviewing a similar annexation undertaken voluntarily might well conclude that such an annexation area did not "abut directly on the municipal boundary."[22] Is there any way to predict what sorts of areas might create difficulties, or how much contiguity is necessary to overcome those difficulties?

The shoestring annexations present the easier case. In *Amick*, as in the shoestring cases from other states, the real target of the annexation was at some considerable distance from the city, and the shoestring was the necessary connection between the city and that real target. When the real target of an annexation is so clearly not contiguous to the city, nor is even close to being contiguous, the court's refusal to uphold the annexation is not surprising. Adding a few feet to the width of the shoestring will not change the basic fact that the actual target is in no sense contiguous to the city's boundary. Only when there is some independent reason for annexing the shoestring itself might such an annexation survive a challenge.

Annexations in which the area is contiguous at only a single point are fundamentally different. In these annexations, the tract connected to the city by the single point is usually the real target. Because such a tract is, in fact, contiguous to the city—if only by the smallest of connections—it is not surprising that the case law involving points is less consistent. If a court focuses on the amount of actual contiguity, it might well invalidate such an annexation. But a court that focuses on

---

21. *Id.* at 71, 382 S.E.2d at 226.

22. Of course, this supposition assumes that a plaintiff could somehow get the matter before a court, which—as shown in Volume 1, chapter 7, of this series—would be very difficult. In Town of Seven Devils v. Town of Sugar Mountain, 125 N.C. App. 692, 482 S.E.2d 39 (1997), the court would not allow a challenge to annexation of a shoestring a few feet wide and some 3,430 feet long.

Figure 2.6

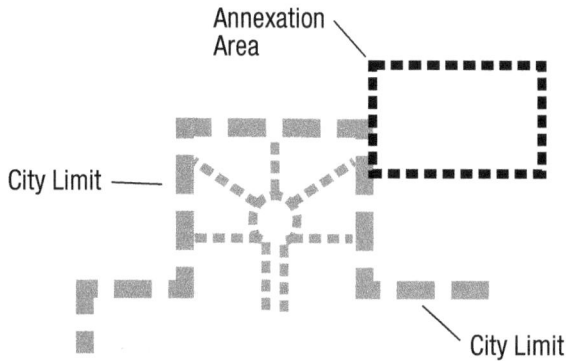

whether the annexation area is, in practical terms, contiguous to the city, might decide that it is and uphold the annexation. Focusing on practical contiguity also avoids the difficulty of determining how much actual contiguity is enough. For example, if the annexation example diagrammed in Figure 2-3(A) were shifted so that there was a larger area of overlap between the annexation area and the existing city limits (*see* Figure 2.6), how much additional overlap would be necessary? A foot, ten feet, twenty-five feet, one hundred feet? No matter which distance is selected, the basic contiguity between the annexation area and the city would be unchanged.

Section 2.07. Annexation across Roads, Streams, Easements, and Publicly Owned Lands

[a] Introduction

As quoted at the beginning of this chapter, G.S. 160A-31(f) considers property contiguous to an annexing city when it is separated from the city's boundary by

- a street or street right-of-way,
- a creek or river,
- the right-of-way of a railroad or other public service corporation,
- lands owned by the city or some other political subdivision, or
- lands owned by the State of North Carolina.

This section explores this form of contiguity.

[b] Across these lands and not along them

A few North Carolina cities have interpreted the language of the statute as allowing a contiguous annexation to proceed *along* a street or a river rather than *across* the street or river. Thus, such a city might try to annex a subdivision a mile from the current city limits and claim that the subdivision is contiguous because it lies along a river that runs from the city limits to the subdivision; or it could annex a commercial development a mile from the current city limits and claim that the development is contiguous because it lies on a street that runs from the city limits to the development. The property being annexed, these cities claim, is "separated from the municipal boundary" by a street or by a river, as the statute provides. Such an interpretation, however, clearly misreads the statute.

The interpretation misuses the purpose of the statutory language. The statutory definition of contiguity begins by defining a contiguous property as one that directly abuts the current city boundary. In the absence of the additional language about streets, rivers, easements, and the like, one might argue that a city could not voluntarily annex a parcel that lies just across a state road from the current city or just across a small stream or a utility easement.[23] The obvious purpose of the additional language is to include those kinds of parcels within the definition of contiguous parcels and to make it clear that such narrow ribbons of land or water have no significance as obstacles to annexation. A property across the road from the city is essentially contiguous in fact, and the statute simply makes that clear. A property a mile down the road from the city is essentially *not* contiguous, and the statutory language is not intended to magically make it so. If property a mile along a street or road or a mile along a river were considered contiguous under the statutory language, then so would any parcel that lies along that road or river, regardless of how far it is from the city. Thus Wilmington might annex a "contiguous" parcel lying along Interstate 40 in Wake County, because the parcel is separated from the city by a street or road; or Elkin could annex a "contiguous" parcel lying along the Yadkin River in Davidson County, because the parcel is separated from the city by a river. The absurdity of those outcomes confirms the absurdity of such a statutory interpretation.

---

23. A court would be likely to find such a parcel contiguous anyway—*see, e.g.,* Beaufort County v. Trask, 536 S.E.2d 660 (S.C. Ct. App. 2002) (property across river is contiguous)—but the statute removes any doubt.

The case law from other states supports the idea that the statute intends *across* rather than *along* streets, rivers, easements, and the like. In Oregon, the annexation statute permits contiguous annexation of territory that is "separated from [the city] only by a public right of way." The city of St. Helens attempted to annex a tract on which a Wal-Mart store was to be built and that was separated from the city by 1,500 feet of road right-of-way. In *Department of Land Conservation and Development v. City of St. Helens,*[24] the Oregon court of appeals disallowed the annexation, holding that the statute permits annexation with only a *"minimal* amount of intervening land of the described kind"—that is, of road right-of-way.[25] In *People ex rel. Adamowski v. Village of Streamwood,*[26] the village had attempted to annex seventy-five miles of roadways radiating out from the current village limits, arguing that these roadways were contiguous to the village. The Illinois court responded as follows:

> The word "contiguous," as used in [the annexation] statute, must be defined in keeping with what was the obvious intention of the legislature, which was to make it permissible for a municipality to annex a roadway where, for example, a roadway separates a municipality from territory just the other side of the roadway, which the municipality needs for existing municipal purposes and for natural growth, even though no part of the roadway lies within the municipality. Contiguous, for any reasonable interpretation of [the statute], must mean contiguous in the sense of adjacent to and parallel to the existing municipal limits and cannot, under any circumstances, permit a municipality by annexation ordinances to grab a whole maze of roadways.[27]

---

24. 907 P.2d 259 (Or. Ct. App. 1995).

25. *Id.* at 262.

26. 155 N.E.2d 635 (Ill. 1959).

27. *Id.* at 638. In one case, however, a court took the opposing view. Georgia's law, like North Carolina's, defines property as contiguous if it is separated from the city by a street or road right-of-way. In City of Gainesville v. Hall County Board of Education, 209 S.E.2d 637 (Ga. 1974), the city had gone out along a series of highways to annex properties at some distance from the city, justifying the annexations as contiguous within the statutory language. In a divided decision, the supreme court of Georgia agreed, holding that to limit contiguity to property across a road from the city would be to deprive the property owner a "free election as to whether to have [his or her property] within or without the municipality." *Id.* at 640.

[c] Intervening property

G.S. 160A-31(f) provides that in "describing the area to be annexed in the annexation ordinance, the municipal governing board *may* include within the description any territory described in this subsection which separates the municipal boundary from the area petitioning for annexation." Despite the statutory use of the verb *may*, the court of appeals has held that this intervening territory (i.e., streets, rivers, railroad rights-of-way, etc.) automatically becomes part of the city along with the property described in the petition. In *Town of Valdese v. Burke, Inc.*,[28] Valdese voluntarily annexed an area lying on the other side of the Interstate 40 right-of-way from the current town limits. Two years earlier, however, the General Assembly had annexed that right-of-way to the neighboring town of Rutherford College by legislative act. The court of appeals invalidated the Valdese annexation on the ground that when the town annexed the property across the interstate, it also annexed the intervening interstate right-of-way. "According to the plain language of G.S. 160A-31(f)," the court said, "when a municipality skips over public lands or rights-of-way in the course of annexing taxable and serviceable property on the other side, the annexing municipality, in effect, annexes the intervening public lands and rights-of-way." [29] Because that intervening right-of-way was already in another town, the Valdese annexation failed because one town cannot annex property already in another.

The court's interpretation of the statutory effect is sensible and does not in fact do violence to the statutory language. If annexing property across a road automatically brings into the city the intervening road as well as the property beyond it, the statutory language simply makes it clear that the city may include that section of the road in the description of the annexed area to recognize that fact. That is, the statutory language is not permission to the city to *annex* the intervening road but simply permission to *describe* the intervening road as part of the annexation. The road is annexed, though, whether the ordinance description includes it or not.[30]

---

28. 125 N.C. App. 688, 482 S.E.2d 24 (1997).

29. *Id.* at 691, 482 S.E.2d at 25.

30. Some cities' annexation petition forms state that the annexation includes all intervening roads, rights-of-way, and the like; thus the petition includes the intervening property.

[d] Intervening property within an annexation area

The statute provides that property is contiguous to the city when it is separated from the city by a street, river, railroad or utility easement, or public property. If such property lies *within* the annexation area, it probably retains its character as intervening property there as well, thus maintaining the internal contiguity of the proposed annexation area. For example, if a proposed annexation area is split by a stream or a railroad track, the land on both sides would be considered contiguous to each other and could therefore be appropriately included in the same annexation proceeding. Although this point is not addressed by the annexation statute, and has not been the subject of appellate litigation in North Carolina, this interpretation maintains a consistent treatment of these intervening strips. In addition, it is supported by decisions from other jurisdictions. For example, in *Common Council of City of Gloversville v. Town Board of Town of Johnstown*,[31] the New York annexation statute required that the annexation area "adjoin" the city. In *Gloverville* the annexation area in question did adjoin the city on one side but was bisected by a state highway. Johnstown—which sought to void the annexation to the city—argued that the property on the far side of the highway did not adjoin the city. The New York court of appeals disagreed, holding that the property on both sides of the highway was a single annexation area and did in fact adjoin the city.

[e] Different kinds of intervening property

The statute mentions the following kinds of intervening properties.

A street or street right-of-way. The statutory language includes property on the other side of an interstate or other limited-access highway, even though there is no direct access across such a highway from the city to the annexation area, and therefore city employees might have to leave the city in order to reach the annexation area to provide services. This conclusion is clear from the court's holding in *Town of Valdese v. Burke, Inc.* (described in section 2.07[c]). There, the court noted that the town would have successfully annexed across the interstate had the right-of-way not already been within another town. Decisions from other states support this understanding of the North

---

31. 295 N.E.2d 644 (N.Y. 1973).

Carolina statute.[32] There is no reason to think that the statute does not apply to private streets or roads as well as to publicly maintained ones.

A creek or a river. The statutory language probably also includes property on the other side of the Intracoastal Waterway from a city. In most places, the Waterway is no wider than many rivers, and the annexing city will usually be the most appropriate provider of municipal services to the property in question.

Property on the other side of a lake may be more problematic, even if the lake is artificial and lies along the watershed of a river or creek. The purpose of the statutory language defining contiguity as including properties separated from the city by various categories of intervening lands or water is to permit annexation of functionally contiguous properties. Property that is separated from the city by a sizable lake— Lake Norman to use a prominent example—will often not be contiguous in any functional sense, and a court might easily decide that the property is not contiguous in a legal sense either. Property across a smaller lake, on the other hand, might be clearly contiguous in a functional sense, and a court might be more likely to uphold a town's annexation of it.

The right-of-way of a railroad or other public service corporation. Note that it's only rights-of-way that are included in the listing of intervening lands. Land owned by a railroad or other public service corporation in fee simple and used for a purpose other than a right-of-way—such as a railroad station or switching yard or a power-generating plant—cannot be considered intervening property.

The meaning of *railroad* is clear, but the term *public service corporation* is not defined in the annexation statute, nor in any other North Carolina statute.[33] Two statutes, however, use the term in a context that provides examples that may indicate how the term is used in the annexation statute. Under G.S. 104-14, the United States, or the state acting on behalf of the United States, can condemn land for the Intracoastal Waterway, even if the property is being used by "a railroad

---

32. *E.g.,* May v. Lee County, 483 So.2d 481 (Fla. Ct. App. 1986); People *ex rel.* Village of South Barrington v. Village of Hoffman Estates, 198 N.E.2d 97 (Ill. 1964).

33. Article 23 of G.S 105 contains special provisions for valuing the property of *public service companies*, which are defined in G.S. 105-333. Perhaps the annexation statute meant for public service *corporation* to have the same meaning as public service *company*, but it could easily have used the same term if that were so. In any event, public service *companies* include airlines and motor freight companies, neither of which is likely to own rights-of-way; and so perhaps the tax term is overly inclusive.

company, a street railway company, telephone or telegraph company, or *other public service corporation*" (emphasis added). Similarly, G.S. 75-9 authorizes the attorney general to investigate possible restraints of trade by "corporations . . . engaged . . . in the business of transporting property or passengers, or transmitting messages, and all *other public service corporations*" (emphasis added). From these statutes, we can see that public service corporations include railroad and street railroad companies, motor freight companies, telephone companies, and telegraph companies. In addition, the state supreme court has defined electrical transmission and distribution companies as public service corporations;[34] by analogy, we can extend the term to include natural gas pipelines and distribution companies and water and sewer utilities. Functionally, such a list makes sense within the terms of the statute because all the types of corporation listed, except motor freight carriers, normally own and use rights-of-way as a core part of their business.

Lands owned by a political subdivision or by the State of North Carolina. The preceding kinds of intervening lands are essentially narrow strips that divide the current city from the property being annexed. But land that is owned by the state or a local government could well be much more extensive and create considerable real separation between the annexing city and the property seeking annexation. By including government-owned lands in the list of intervening properties, the statute may recognize that prohibiting annexation across such lands might impede the otherwise natural growth of a city or deny property owners needed municipal services. Nonetheless, when a city attempts a contiguous annexation across a sizable tract of local government–owned or state-owned property, there is always the danger that a court might ignore the literal language of the statute and find that the property is not in fact contiguous.

34. Whiting Manufacturing Co. v. Carolina Aluminum Co., 207 N.C. 52, 175 S.E. 698 (1934).

Standards for Satellite Annexations

Standards for Satellite Annexations

Section 3.01. Introduction

[a] History

In 1967 the General Assembly passed local legislation giving the city of Raleigh permission to annex noncontiguous areas up to three miles from its existing city limits.[1] These noncontiguous areas were quickly labeled "satellites" of the primary city, and this form of annexation became known as satellite annexation. During the next four years, the General Assembly gave comparable authority to Fayetteville and Benson, and it added seven more cities in 1973.[2] In 1974 the General Assembly enacted general legislation granting all North Carolina cities authority to undertake voluntary satellite annexations. Most of the important provisions in the statewide statute can be traced back to the original Raleigh legislation.[3]

[b] Annexing territory to a satellite

As noted in section 2.02, a city may not use the *contiguous* annexation procedure to voluntarily annex territory that abuts an existing satellite area (unless, of course, the area also abuts the city's primary corporate limits). To undertake such an annexation, a city must use the satellite annexation procedure. (See chapter 2 for discussion of this issue.)

1. 1967 N.C. Sess. Laws ch. 989.
2. 1969 N.C. Sess. Laws ch. 715 (Fayetteville); 1971 N.C. Sess. Laws ch. 623 (Benson); 1973 N.C. Sess. Laws ch. 36 (Wilmington), ch. 112 (Nashville), ch. 164 (Selma), ch. 188 (Kure Beach), ch. 375 (Rocky Mount), ch. 427 (Jacksonville), and ch. 651 (Carolina Beach).
3. There is one important exception. The Raleigh legislation, as well as that for Fayetteville, permitted city residents to petition for a referendum on any proposed satellite annexation. None of the other local acts included such a provision, and it was not included in the statewide legislation.

[c] The five standards

Cities undertake satellite annexations pursuant to Part 4 of Article 4A of General Statute Chapter 160A (hereinafter G.S.), beginning with G.S. 160A-58. The five standards a satellite annexation must meet are set out in G.S. 160A-58.1(b) as follows:

1. Some part of the annexation area must be within three miles of the annexing city's primary corporate limits.
2. No point in the annexation area may be closer to the primary corporate limits of another city than to the primary corporate limits of the annexing city.
3. The annexing city must be able to provide the same services to the annexation area that it provides to areas within its primary corporate limits.
4. If the area is a subdivision, the entire subdivision must be annexed.
5. The total area of a city's satellites may not exceed 10 percent of the area within its primary corporate limits.

The remaining sections of this chapter review each of these five standards in turn.

Section 3.02. Distance from Primary Corporate Limits

The nearest point on the proposed satellite corporate limits must be not more than three miles from the primary corporate limits of the annexing city.[4]

This standard is straightforward and only rarely occasions difficulty. The General Assembly has decided that while annexing satellite areas does no violence to the notion of a city as a single, relatively compact entity, those areas must not be too far from the city's primary limits.[5] Three points should be made about this standard.

4. Section 160A-58.1(b)(1) of the North Carolina General Statutes (hereinafter, G.S.).
5. See the discussion in Hawks v. Town of Valdese, 299 N.C. 1, 12-13, 261 S.E.2d 90, 97 (1980) ("Contiguity, then, is an essential component of the traditional concept of a municipal corporation, which is envisioned as a governmental unit capable of providing essential governmental services to residents within compact borders. . . . [T]o permit

Figure 3.1

Primary
City Limit   Existing
              Satellite Area   Proposed
                                      Satellite Area

2.98 miles

3.02 miles

Proposed satellite is not
within 3 miles of primary
city limits.

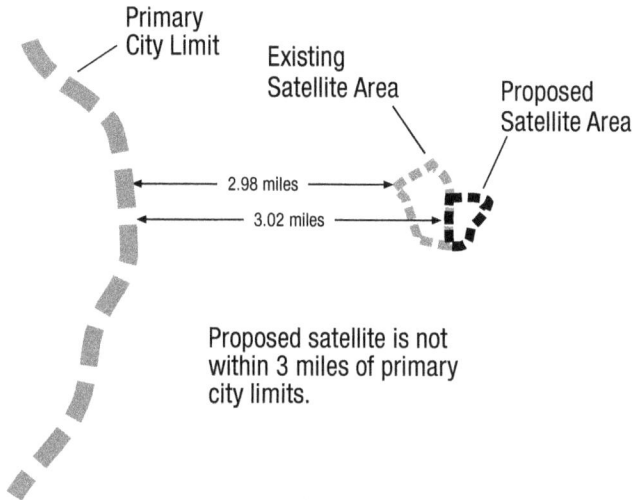

First, the standard does not require the entire annexation area to be within three miles of the primary limits—only the point of the area that is closest to the annexing city.

Second, if a city is using the satellite procedure to annex an area contiguous to an existing satellite area, the distance must still be measured from the primary corporate limits and not from the satellite limits. If part of the existing satellite area is more than three miles from the city's corporate limits, and if the proposed satellite area abuts that far side of the existing satellite area, the city will not be able to under-take the annexation until the primary limits expand further toward the satellite area (*see* Figure 3.1).

Third, although G.S. 160A-58.7 sets out a procedure under which a city may annex city-owned property as a satellite, it stipulates that such an annexation must still meet the standards of G.S. 160A-58.1(b). Therefore, if a city-owned tract is more than three miles from the primary corporate limits, it cannot be annexed with the satellite procedure—or any other statutory procedure.

---

cities to evolve into a number of diverse, noncontiguous town areas is to invite financial and political instability into the structure of municipal government.").

Section 3.03. Proximity to Another City's Primary Limits

No point on the proposed satellite corporate limits may be closer to the primary corporate limits of another city than to the primary corporate limits of the annexing city, except as set forth in subsection (b2) of this section.[6]

[a] In general

Four points should be made about this second standard.

First, this standard embodies the state's basic policy that only the city that is closest to it may annex a proposed satellite area, even though the occasional result is a satellite area that no city may legally annex. This can occur when one point of a satellite area is closer to City A but another point is closer to City B (as illustrated in Figure 3.2). As long as none of the relevant boundaries is changed, neither city can annex that satellite area.

Second, the statute does not empower the city that is closest to the satellite area to waive this standard and allow the other city's annexation to go forward. The standard is not intended specifically to protect that city but rather to define the appropriate limits of satellite annexation. If the closer city does not oppose the annexation, however, the annexing city can ask the General Assembly to either waive the standard in this instance or annex the area to it by legislative annexation.

Third, the standard applies even if the city that is closer is unable or unwilling to provide the city services that are needed or desired by the owners of the property seeking annexation. If that is the case, the only way to effect the annexation would be, again, to ask the General Assembly to waive the standard for that proposed annexation or legislate the annexation directly.

Fourth, the standard applies only when the closer city is a North Carolina city and not a city in some other state. Although there are areas in North Carolina that are closer to a city in another state than to any North Carolina city, those non–North Carolina cities are not legally entitled to annex or provide city services to the North Carolina areas. These cities' proximity to such a proposed annexation area is therefore irrelevant to the legal capacity of a North Carolina city to annex the area.

6. G.S. 160A-58.1(b)(2).

Figure 3.2

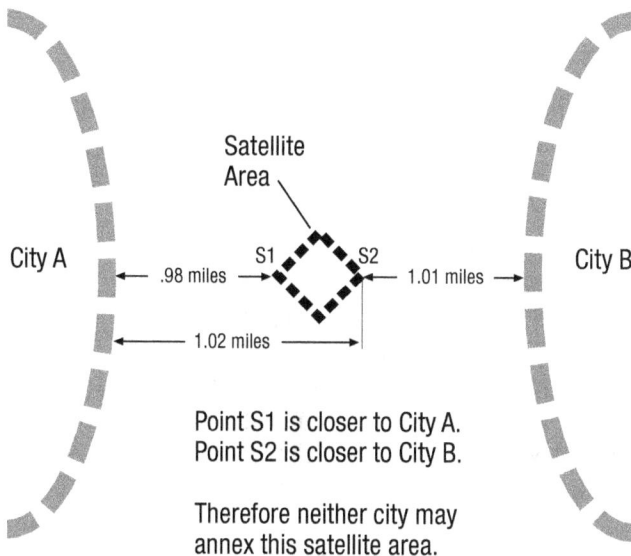

Satellite Area

City A   S1   S2   City B
← .98 miles →   ← 1.01 miles →

← 1.02 miles →

Point S1 is closer to City A.
Point S2 is closer to City B.

Therefore neither city may
annex this satellite area.

[b] The exception

If two or more cities have entered into an annexation agreement under which each city has a sphere of influence within which only it may annex, the standard discussed in this section might not apply.[7] If a proposed satellite annexation area is within one city's exclusive sphere of influence, it may annex the area, even if the area is closer to another city, as long as that other city is party to the annexation agreement and is prohibited by the agreement from annexing the area.[8] (The annexation area must still meet the other standards set out in G.S. 160A-58.1[b].)

---

7. Annexation agreements are described in Volume 1 of this series, in sections 3.11–17.

8. G.S. 160A-58.1(b2).

Section 3.04. Providing City Services
to Satellite Annexations

The area must be so situated that the annexing city will be able to provide the same services within the proposed satellite corporate limits that it provides within its primary corporate limits.[9]

This standard includes two elements—an objective entitlement of the property owner and a subjective judgment by the city council.

G.S. 160A-58.3 entitles owners of property in an area that has been annexed as a satellite to "the same privileges and benefits as other parts of the city." That is, the statute requires that the city provide a satellite area with the same services as areas within the primary limits of the city, consistent with whatever policies the city has for providing those services. If a city is for some reason unable to deliver one or more city services to the satellite area, then it cannot meet this standard and should not annex the property. This is true even if the property owner does not care about receiving the service in question and is in fact willing to sign some sort of waiver regarding it. As discussed in Volume 1, section 4.06[b], the city probably could not enforce such a waiver against the property owner who gives it—and certainly not against any subsequent owner of the property.

The situation in which a city is unable to provide a city service to a satellite annexation area is probably rare. Nonetheless, this standard could cause a city council to decide against annexing a proposed satellite area if it believed that the expense of providing city services to the area does not justify the annexation. That is, this standard is at least partially intended to cause the city council to weigh the advantages and disadvantages of the proposed annexation, particularly the city's service costs relative to the revenues it would derive from the annexed property (and any other difficulties the city might face in providing services to the annexed area).

9. G.S. 160A-58.1(b)(3).

Section 3.05. Annexing a Subdivision

If the area proposed for annexation, or any portion thereof, is a subdivision as defined in G.S. 160A-376, all of the subdivision must be included.[10]

[a] The basic meaning of this requirement

The accepted understanding. The usual understanding of this fourth standard is as follows: If any part of the proposed annexation area is within a platted subdivision, the entire subdivision must be included within the annexation. A city may not split a subdivision and annex only part of it. Although this standard has not been the subject of an appellate decision, it was involved in two cases that did reach the appellate courts and in which all parties and the judges understood the standard in the way set out above.

In *City of Burlington v. Town of Elon College*,[11] Elon College had attempted a satellite annexation of certain areas included in an involuntary annexation being undertaken by Burlington. The record on appeal includes an affidavit from Elon College's consulting engineer concluding that the areas met the five standards for satellite annexation. With respect to this standard, his affidavit read: "No areas constitute splitting of a subdivision."[12]

In *Joyner v. Town of Weaverville*,[13] the plaintiffs attacked the town's satellite annexation on the ground that the annexation did split a subdivision. The city didn't disagree with the plaintiffs' reading of the statute but only with their contention that the annexation split a subdivision. The trial court ruled for the city, but the court of appeals decided the case by denying standing to the plaintiffs and so never ruled on the subdivision issue.

An alternative reading. Although the understanding of the standard stated above is widely accepted, some observers have proposed an alternative meaning based on a carefully parsed reading of the statute. These people point out that if the clause separated by commas is

---

10. G.S. 160A-58.1(b)(4).
11. 310 N.C. 723, 314 S.E.2d 534 (1984).
12. *Id.,* record at 28.
13. 94 N.C. App. 588, 380 S.E.2d 536 (1989).

removed, the standard reads "If the area proposed for annexation . . . is a subdivision as defined in G.S. 160A-376, all of the subdivision must be included." They emphasize that the standard begins "if the area proposed . . ." and argue that the standard should be limited to that situation. That is, if the petition proposes an annexation area that is a subdivision, the entire subdivision must be annexed. But they also infer from the "if" clause that petitioners are free to propose an area that is only part of a subdivision; and in that case the standard simply does not apply, because the area that is proposed is *not* a subdivision. If the clause between the commas is reinserted into the standard, supporters of the alternative reading argue that the clause refers back to "the area proposed for annexation," so that the clause might be rewritten to read "or if any portion of the area proposed for annexation" is a subdivision. That is, *if* the area proposed by petitioners includes an entire sub-division as well as other property, the entire subdivision must be included in the annexation.

The purpose of the provision, according to this reading, is to ensure that if the petitioners propose the annexation of an entire subdivision, the city council may not include less than that entire subdivision in the final annexation area. But, to repeat, the standard does not, on this reading, require petitioners to propose annexation of the entire subdivision but rather is triggered only if they do so.

Analysis of the alternative reading. There are two difficulties with this alternative reading. First, it assumes that a city council has the discretion to annex some rather than all of the area proposed for annexation, but that is not true. G.S. 160A-58.2 authorizes the annexing city to respond to a satellite annexation petition by adopting "an ordinance annexing *the area described in the petition.*" There is no authority in the statute to annex a lesser area than that described in the petition. In *Conover v. Newton,*[14] the North Carolina supreme court examined comparable language in the voluntary annexation statute and held that a city must either annex the entire area proposed for annex-ation or none of it. Thus, the alternative reading ends up making the standard meaningless because the council cannot reduce the area to be annexed in any event.

Second, the alternative reading assumes that the five standards bind only the city council as it determines whether to annex the proposed

14. 297 N.C. 506, 256 S.E.2d 216 (1979).

area. But in fact they bind the petitioners as well. The opening language of G.S. 160A-58.1(b) states that a satellite area "proposed for annexation must meet all" the five standards. The only way the subdivision standard makes sense in that case is to read it to say that if the proposed annexation area includes any part of a subdivision, it must include the entire subdivision. Otherwise the standard is tautological, viz.: if the proposed annexation area includes an entire subdivision, it must include the entire subdivision. If the first is true, the second is obviously true, and the standard serves no purpose. If, then, it is to serve any purpose, it must be understood in the commonly accepted way.

The accepted understanding also follows the original model for the satellite annexation statute, Raleigh's 1967 local act permitting that city to undertake satellite annexations. That local act clearly (although somewhat awkwardly) required the city to annex an entire subdivision or none of it. The relevant paragraph in the local act read:

> In the case of annexing a subdivision under this Act, the petition must be signed by all owners of property within the subdivision; provided nothing herein shall be construed to authorize the annexation of a portion of a subdivision.

It is much more likely that the drafters of the 1974 statewide statute intended to carry forward the policy set out in the local acts for Raleigh and most of the other cities than to significantly modify that policy.

Finally, the accepted understanding makes sense as a policy. Allowing satellite annexation at all is a departure from the general notion of the city as a compact, contiguous entity. The General Assembly might appropriately have concluded that if satellites were to be allowed at all, it was better to annex entire subdivisions than scattered lots within a subdivision. A city can more easily meet the burdens of providing city services and more rationally regulate land use in an entire subdivision than in scattered lots. Furthermore, modern subdivisions commonly create a homeowners' association to provide internal governance and services; annexing only part of a subdivision might well disrupt such an association's service responsibilities.

[b] What is a subdivision?

The satellite annexation statute prohibits division of a subdivision "as defined in G.S. 160A-376." That definition reads as follows:

> "Subdivision" means all divisions of a tract or parcel of land into two or more lots, building sites, or other divisions for the purpose of sale or building development (whether immediate or future) and shall include all divisions of land involving the dedication of a new street or a change in existing streets.

The statute goes on to list four exceptions to this definition, one of which is relevant to annexations. This relevant exception excludes from the definition "the division of land into parcels greater than 10 acres where no street right-of-way dedication is involved."[15] Thus, if a larger parcel has been divided into lots larger than ten acres and no street has been dedicated, a city may annex any one or more of the lots without having to annex all of them.

Some local governments have added to their subdivision ordinances exceptions beyond the four set out in the statutes. (The county sub-division statute, G.S. 153A-335, has the same definition and the same four exceptions as the city statute.) For example, some local governments do not regulate subdivisions of land into lots of five (rather than ten) acres when specified conditions are met. These local exceptions, however, which exempt qualifying divisions of land from local regulation, do not affect the satellite annexation statute. Even if a particular division of land has been exempted from regulation by such a locally adopted exception, it may not be divided in a satellite annexation if it meets the General Statutes' definition. This is true even if the local variation has been specifically authorized by a local act of the General Assembly. The annexation statute references the general law definition.

It should also be noted that the statutory definition is limited to divisions of land undertaken "for the purpose of sale or building development." If land is divided for some other purpose, the result is not a subdivision for purposes of the definition and therefore is not one for purposes of satellite annexation. For example, in *Williamson v. Avant*,[16] the court of appeals in 1974 held that a division of land for the purpose of dividing real estate among heirs to settle an estate did not meet the comparable definition of subdivision in the then-current statute authorizing counties to regulate subdivisions. Because such a

15. G.S. 160A-376(2). See Three Guys Real Estate v. Harnett County, 345 N.C. 468, 480 S.E.2d 681 (1997), in which the supreme court held that a county could not regulate a subdivision that fell within this exception.
16. 21 N.C. App. 211, 203 S.E.2d 634 (1974).

division of land was not subject to county regulation, it would not have qualified as a subdivision under the terms of the satellite annexation statute either.

This satellite annexation standard also *does not* apply when the owner of a large tract of land that is not otherwise part of a subdivision petitions for annexation of a portion of the tract. Such a petition does not subdivide the tract into smaller parcels; it just seeks to run a municipal boundary down the middle of it. Simply annexing part of a tract of land into a city and leaving part outside does not, in and of itself, divide that tract into two smaller parcels.

[c] Phased subdivisions

An owner of a large tract of land who seeks to subdivide and develop the tract sometimes does so in phases. Each phase is separately platted, separately approved, and separately developed, even though master covenants may tie all the phases together. When the standard requires that an entire subdivision be annexed, is it referring to each separate phase or to all the phases together?

It is most likely that the statute is referring to each separate phase as a subdivision. Although the phases may share common master covenants, they are normally subject to separate regulatory approval, are developed at different times, and usually have separate sets of covenants in addition to the master covenants. Often each phase will have its own homeowners' association. Because they are separately approved, phases are treated as separate subdivisions in G.S. 160A-376—the source of the annexation law definition of subdivision. It therefore also makes linguistic sense to treat them as separate subdivisions in interpreting the annexation law. Furthermore, the various purposes the statutory standard is designed to fulfill—efficient provision of city services, more rational land use regulation, and smooth functioning of homeowners' associations—are each satisfied by treating phases as separate subdivisions.[17]

---

17. The annexation challenged in Joyner v. Town of Weaverville, 94 N.C. App. 588, 380 S.E.2d 536 (1989), involved the first phase of a phased subdivision; the challengers argued that the entire eventual development, not just the first phase, ought to have been annexed. The trial court upheld the annexation, but the court of appeals decided the case on other grounds.

Section 3.06. Limiting the Area of a City's Satellite Annexations

The area within the proposed satellite corporate limits, when added to the area within all other satellite corporate limits, may not exceed ten percent (10%) of the area within the primary corporate limits of the annexing city.[18]

This final standard is straightforward and furthers the apparent legislative goal of not allowing satellite annexations to undermine significantly the notion of a city as a single, contiguous, and compact entity. In practice, however, the standard has proved to be a problem for many smaller cities, because one large development by itself may easily exceed the 10-percent limit.[19] If that development is a unitary subdivision and is not developed in phases, the 10-percent limit may block the satellite annexation altogether. Because of this and similar problems, the General Assembly has excepted a significant number of cities from this 10-percent standard by local act.[20]

18. G.S. 160A-58.1(b)(5).

19. The satellite annexation being challenged in Joyner v. Town of Weaverville, 94 N.C. App. 588, 380 S.E.2d 536 (1989), was limited to the first stages of a single development because the entire development would have exceeded the 10-percent limit. *Joyner*, record at 42–43.

20. The cities that have gained exemptions from the 10-percent limit are included in Table 1.2 in Volume 1, chapter 1 of this series.

4

Petition Requirements

Petition Requirements

Section 4.01. Introduction

Section 160A-31 of the North Carolina General Statutes (hereinafter G.S.), the contiguous annexation statute, requires that the annexation petition be signed "by the owners of all the real property located within [the annexation] area," while G.S. 160A-58.1, the satellite statute, uses almost identical language to impose the same requirement. This chapter begins by discussing a number of substantive issues concerned with the annexation petition, moves on to a description of certain procedural matters concerning the petition, and concludes by outlining the procedure to be followed when the city itself owns the property being annexed.

Section 4.02. Owners Who Need Not Sign the Satellite Petition

[a] Introduction

Although G.S. 160A-58.1(a) begins by requiring a satellite annexation petition to be signed "by all of the owners of real property" in the annexation area, in the next sentence it states that the petition "need not be signed" by certain categories of owners. The categories are:

- owners of property "wholly exempt from property taxation,"
- railroad companies,
- public utilities, and
- electric or telephone membership companies.

[b] Property exempt from taxation

The precise language of G.S. 160A-58.1(a) is that the petition need not be signed "by the owners of real property that is wholly exempt from property taxation under the Constitution and laws of North Carolina." The word *exemption* is a term of art in North Carolina property tax law, and *exempt* property in the technical sense does not include all property that is exempt from taxation in the popular sense. A first issue about this provision of the satellite annexation statute is therefore whether it uses the term *exempt* in its technical or its popular sense.

Article V, section 2(3) of the North Carolina Constitution is entitled "Exemptions" and includes the following language:

> Property belonging to the State, counties, and municipal corporations shall be exempt from taxation. The General Assembly may exempt cemeteries and property held for educational, scientific, literary, cultural, charitable, or religious purposes[.]

Article V, section 2(2) of the Constitution is entitled "Classification" and says, in part, that "[o]nly the General Assembly shall have the power to classify property for taxation[.]" When the General Assembly wishes to treat a category of property differently for property tax purposes, it *classifies* the category and then applies the special treatment. A common form of special treatment is to exclude the category of property from the tax base.

Property may therefore avoid taxation because it is *exempt,* either by the constitution or by statute; in addition, it may avoid taxation because it has been *classified and excluded* from the tax base by statute.[1] In either case, the whole value of the property escapes taxation, and both sorts of property are exempt in the popular sense. In constitutional terminology, however, only the first sort is technically exempt. Therefore, the question arises, does a satellite petition need to be signed by the owner of property that has been classified and excluded from the property tax base? Or is that property included within the statutory category of property that is "wholly exempt" from taxation, making its owner's signature unnecessary? (Table 4.1 sets out the kinds of properties that are *exempt* from taxation under the state constitution or statutes, while Table 4.2 describes properties that have been classified and excluded from taxation by statute.)

---

1. G.S. 105-274 states that all property is subject to taxation except (1) property that has been "excluded from the tax base . . . [as] enacted under the classification power," or (2) property that has been "exempted from taxation by the Constitution or by a statute" authorized by the Constitution.

Table 4.1

Categories of Real Property
Wholly Exempt from Taxation

Category	Statute
Government property owned by	
the United States government	G.S. 105-278.1(a)
the state or local government	G.S. 105-278.1(b)
Religious or educational property owned by	
a religious organization and used for religious purposes	G.S. 105-278.3
a nonprofit educational institution and used for educational purposes	G.S. 105-278.4
a religious educational assembly and used for religious purposes or religious education	G.S. 105-278.5
Charitable property owned by	
a YMCA or similar organization	G.S. 105-278.6(a)(1)
a home for the aged, sick, or infirm	G.S. 105-278.6(a)(2)
an orphanage or similar home	G.S. 105-278.6(a)(3)
the ASPCA or similar society	G.S. 105-278.6(a)(4)
a reformatory or correctional institution	G.S. 105-278.6(a)(5)
a monastery, convent, or nunnery	G.S. 105-278.6(a)(6)
a nonprofit rescue squad	G.S. 105-278.6(a)(7)
a nonprofit organization providing affordable housing	G.S. 105-278.6(a)(8)
a charitable organization and used for educational, scientific, literary, or charitable purposes	G.S. 105-278.7
a hospital organized and operated as a nonprofit, charitable organization and used for hospital purposes	G.S. 105-278.8
Cemetery property	
not held for sale or for sale of burial rights	G.S. 105-278.2

Table 4.2

Categories of Real Property Classified and
Wholly Excluded from Taxation

Category	Statute
Property providing public services	
and owned by	
a nonprofit water or sewer association	G.S. 105-275(3)
a nonprofit corporation or other charitable organization and used exclusively for a public parks and drives	G.S. 105-275(7)
a nonprofit corporation created to finance public facilities leased to the state or a local government and used for public purposes	G.S. 105-275(39)
Property serving environmental purposes	
and used	
for air or water pollution abatement, reduction, or prevention	G.S. 105-275(8)a.
for recycling or resource recovery of or from solid waste	G.S. 105-275(8)b.
as a "major recycling facility"	G.S. 105-275(8)d.
Property owned by a nonprofit organization	
and used as a protected natural area	G.S. 105-275(12)
Standing timber	
and other forest growth	G.S. 105-275(15)
Property owned by lodges and similar organizations	
and used by	
veterans' organizations for meetings	G.S. 105-275(17)
specific Masonic organizations for meetings	G.S. 105-275(18)
fraternal or civic organizations for meetings	G.S. 105-275(19)
Property owned by Goodwill Industries and comparable organizations	
and used	
for the training and rehabilitation of disabled persons	G.S. 105-275(20)

Table 4.2 (continued)

Category	Statute
Property used in historic preservation	
Property held and exclusively used by a nonprofit historic preservation organization for nonprofit historic preservation purposes	G.S. 105-275(29)
Property in a historic district and owned by a nonprofit corporation organized for historic preservation purposes and held for use as a future site for a historic structure to be moved to the site	G.S. 105-275(29a)
Retirement property	
owned and used by a "qualified retirement facility"	G.S. 105-278.6A

From a policy standpoint, it is hard to see why the General Assembly would have provided that the owners of technically exempt property need not sign but not have excepted owners of property classified and excluded from the tax base. Neither form of property is liable for property taxes, so the owners of both forms should be equally indifferent to an annexation. If the General Assembly has classified property and excluded it from the tax base, it can, of course, change its mind and terminate the exclusion. But, as most forms of exemption are also created by statute rather than mandated by the constitution, the General Assembly can also change its mind about an exemption and terminate it. Property that has been classified and excluded may be sold and lose the exclusion, but so can property that is exempt. There thus seems to be no practical difference between exempt property and property that has been classified and excluded that would explain why the annexation statute would draw a distinction between them. It seems more likely that in writing the satellite statute the General Assembly was using the term *exempt* in its popular rather than its technical sense. It would therefore be reasonable for a city presented with a satellite annexation petition for an area that includes property classified and excluded from the tax base to accept and act on it, even if the owner of the classified property has not signed the petition.

[c] Railroads, public utilities, and membership corporations

These businesses share the characteristic of conducting their business along narrow strips of land: rail lines, water lines, sewer lines, electric lines, natural gas pipelines, telephone lines. In most cases, the company holds an easement for these strips of land, rather than the fee simple title; and as Section 4.03[c] (below) argues, owners of easements need not sign annexation petitions in any event. Some companies, however, particularly railroads, do hold fee simple title to their strips and therefore would, if not excluded by the statute, have to sign a petition if the strip crosses the annexation area. The provision allowing petitions not signed by such owners seems intended to allow annexations to go forward without their signature, regardless of the company's ownership interest.

These kinds of companies also own much more substantial parcels of property—railroad terminals and yards, power generating facilities, water or sewerage treatment plants, office facilities, and so on. On its face, the statute also permits cities to include these kinds of properties in a satellite annexation without company signatures. The statute does not, though, allow annexation of such facilities against the wishes of the company in question (as discussed below). If the company objects to such an annexation, the rule enunciated in *County of Brunswick v. Town of Bolivia* (discussed in the next paragraphs of this chapter) permits the company to remove its property from the annexation.

[d] Objections from non-signing property owners

What happens if, pursuant to G.S. 160A-58.1(a), property is included in a satellite annexation without the signature of the owner and that owner does not wish to be included in the annexation? The 1982 case of *County of Brunswick v. Town of Bolivia*[2] suggests that such owners may be able to challenge the annexation and have their property removed from the annexation area. In the early 1980s, Brunswick County moved its county seat from the town of Southport to a 38.5-acre tract in the middle of the county, near the town of Bolivia. The county intentionally established the new center for county facilities at a location outside any of the county's numerous municipalities. Despite the county's intention, the town of Bolivia arranged to be presented with a petition to satellite-annex the county property. The petition was signed

2. 56 N.C. App. 732, 289 S.E.2d 569 (1982).

by a number of residents of the town and the surrounding areas. The county did not sign it—because the property was exempt from taxation—even though the proposed annexation area consisted entirely of county property. When the town proceeded to adopt an ordinance annexing the property over the county's objections, the county brought suit. The trial court held the petition invalid, and the court of appeals affirmed.

The reasoning of the appellate court was limited to the circumstances of that particular case. The court noted that "[n]othing in G.S. 160A-58.1 requires or authorizes the signatures of non-property owners"[3] on an annexation petition; therefore the signatures of all those who did not own property in the annexation area should have been excluded from consideration. Doing that left the petition with *no* signatures, so that there was nothing for the town to consider.

Although this line of reasoning responded to the particular facts in *Brunswick v. Bolivia*, it suggests an interesting possibility. What if a city or town within three miles of an electric power generating facility receives a petition for annexation of a noncontiguous tract containing two parcels—the generating facility and a small parcel that abuts the generating facility—that is signed only by the owner of the small parcel? Although the reasoning of *Brunswick* would not apply to this petition because the petition would contain a signature from an owner of property in the annexation area, it is difficult to believe that a court would allow such an annexation to go forward over the protests of the owners of the generating facility. It is much more likely that a court would point to the outcome of *Brunswick*, as well as the case of *Allman v. City of Newton*,[4] and find a principle that an owner not required to sign a satellite annexation petition can nevertheless object to annexation of its property and force the town to remove it from the annexation area. Otherwise, the signature provision in G.S. 160A-58.1(a) would convert this voluntary annexation procedure into an involuntary one for any owner not required to sign a satellite petition.

3. *Id.* at 733, 289 S.E.2d at 570.

4. 297 N.C. 506, 256 S.E.2d 216 (1979). This case held that persons who sign an annexation petition are entitled to remove their names from the petition up to the time the city adopts the annexation ordinance. This aspect of the case is discussed fully in Book 1 of this series, section 7.04[b], and in section 4.05[b] of this chapter.

Section 4.03. What Ownership Interests Must Sign the Petition?

[a] Introduction

It is a legal commonplace that a single parcel of real property is divisible into a number of separate ownership interests—sticks, so to speak, that make up the bundle of property ownership. Someone will always hold the fee simple interest—the basic ownership interest—but the property might also be subject to utility or road easements, burdened by a deed of trust or other security interest, or leased to a tenant. This section addresses the question of which of these possible property interests is meant when the voluntary statutes require the "owners" of the property to sign the petition.

[b] The fee simple owner

The owner of the fee simple interest (or *fee* interest) must sign the petition, but the owners of other interest need not sign. There is no North Carolina case law on this issue, but the above conclusion conforms to popular understanding of the word *owner* and is consistent with relevant case law from other states. The owner of a fee simple estate—the basic form of real property ownership[5]—is normally understood to be the property's owner. It is reasonable to assume that if legislators had intended holders of other interests in property to sign the annexation petition, they would have explicitly stated this in the statute. Furthermore, cases from other states interpreting statutes requiring property owners to sign various sorts of petitions have generally limited the meaning of *owner* to persons or entities holding fee simple title.[6]

---

5. "The estate of fee simple is the entire and absolute property in land. It is the most extensive estate or interest that can be owned in land." I JAMES A. WEBSTER, Jr., WEBSTER'S REAL ESTATE LAW IN NORTH CAROLINA § 4.1 (5th ed. by Patrick K. Hetrick and James B. McLaughlin, Jr., 1999).

6. *E.g.,* City of Cartersville v. Bartow County Sch. Dist., 243 S.E.2d 293 (Ga. Ct. App. 1978) (lessees and holders of security deeds need not sign annexation petitions, because not owners of the property); Petition of Brandt, 62 N.W.2d 816 (Minn. 1954) (mortgagee need not sign petition to establish drainage district, because not owner of the property); Town of Menasha v. City of Menasha, 168 N.W.2d 161 (Wis. 1969) (holder of road easement need not sign annexation petition, because not owner of property).

[c] Holders of other interests in property

Unlike holders of the fee simple interest in real property, holders of the following interests in property need not sign the annexation petition; nor would their signatures be sufficient in the absence of the fee holder's signature.

Lessees. The cases from other states support the conclusion that lessees are not owners of leased property and therefore do not need to sign the annexation petition; nor can they sign the petition in lieu of the fee simple owner.[7] The one exception to this conclusion is a lessee whose lease extends for an extraordinarily long time; in such a case, a court would probably treat the lessee as the owner.[8]

Holders of Easements. The cases from other states support the conclusion that the holder of an easement is not an owner of property and therefore does not need to sign the annexation petition and cannot sign it in lieu of the fee simple owner.[9] One implication of this conclusion is that when the State of North Carolina holds only an easement for a state road or highway, it may not sign a petition to annex the right-of-way. Only the fee simple owners of the land beneath the right-of-way are owners with the power to sign the petition.[10]

7. Smith v. Improvement Dist. No. 14 of Texarkana, 156 S.W. 455 (Ark. 1913) (holder of ninety-nine-year lease not owner for purposes of signing petition for special assessments); City of Cartersville v. Bartow County Sch. Dist., 243 S.E.2d 293 (Ga. Ct. App. 1978) (lessee not owner for purposes of signing annexation petition); People *ex rel.* James v. Chicago, B. & Q. R. Co., 83 N.E. 219 (Ill. 1907) (lessee not owner for purposes of signing petition to disconnect property from city).

8. Village of St. Bernard v. Kemper, 54 N.E. 267 (Ohio 1899) (holder of ninety-nine-year lease, renewable forever, is owner for purposes of petition for special assessments). In some commercial leases, the lessee has a fee simple interest in leasehold improvements. The land under shopping centers is frequently leased in this way. Because the lessee holds the land by lease, however, such a lessee still should be considered a lessee and not an owner for purposes of signing an annexation petition.

9. Nicholson v. Village of Schaumburg Center, 178 N.E.2d 680 (Ill. Ct. App. 1961) (property owner conveyed fee interest in strip of land to natural gas company for pipeline and retained an easement of access and right to farm the land; held, property owner was no longer owner of strip, because natural gas company held fee, and therefore owner could not sign petition to disconnect strip from city); Citizens for Conservation v. Village of Lake Barrington, 608 N.E.2d 653 (Ill. Ct. App. 1993) (holder of conservation easement not owner for purposes of signing petition to disconnect property from city); Petition of Brandt, 62 N.W.2d 816 (Minn. 1954) (county held easements for two roads; held, not owner for purposes of petition to establish drainage district); Town of Menasha v. City of Menasha, 168 N.W.2d 161 (Wis. 1969) (county held easement for highway; held, not owner for purposes of annexation petition).

10. *See, e.g.,* City of Adel v. Georgia Power Co., 161 S.E.2d 297 (Ga. 1968) (fee holder of road right-of-way must sign annexation petition); Town of Menasha v. City of

Security interests. The cases from other states support the conclusion that a mortgagee (the secured party under a mortgage or deed of trust) is not an owner of property and therefore need not sign the annexation petition and cannot sign the petition in lieu of the fee simple owner.[11]

Option holders. The single case from another state supports the conclusion that the holder of an option to acquire property need not sign the petition.[12] If the option is exercised before the annexation ordinance is adopted, however, the optionee has become the owner and must sign the petition.

[d] Purchaser under a land sale contract

There are two types of contracts that a buyer and seller of real estate might sign as part of the conveyance transaction. The more common type evidences the buyer's offer and the seller's acceptance and is normally fulfilled by closing the sale transaction. Under such a contract, the seller is clearly the owner until the closing and the buyer is the owner only after that point; the buyer's signature is therefore necessary only if the annexation ordinance is adopted after the closing.[13]

The second type of contract is much more unusual in North Carolina, though not unheard of. Under a *land sale contract* the buyer pays the seller for the property over time. The buyer becomes the possessor of the property, but the deed to the property is placed in escrow until final payment is made to the seller; at that time, the deed is delivered to the buyer. Such a transaction is comparable to a lease-purchase of personal property. It is also comparable to a real property conveyance financed by a purchase-money mortgage or deed of trust given to the seller, except that in a purchase-money transaction title is transferred at the closing rather than upon final payment. Under a land sale contract,

---

Menasha, 168 N.W.2d 161 (Wis. 1969) (county held easement for highway; held, not owner for purposes of annexation petition).

11. *E.g.,* Holt v. Ring, 9 S.W.2d 43 (Ark. 1928) (mortgagor proper party to sign special assessment petition); City of Cartersville v. Bartow County Sch. Dist., 243 S.E.2d 293 (Ga. Ct. App. 1978) (holders of security deeds not owners for purposes of signing annexation petitions); Petition of Brandt, 62 N.W.2d 816 (Minn. 1954) (mortgagee is not owner for purposes of signing petition to establish drainage district).

12. Elkins v. City and County of Denver, 402 P.2d 617 (Colo. 1965) (annexation petition).

13. Board of Improvement Dist. No. 5 v. Offenhauser, 105 S.W. 265 (Ark. 1907) (special assessment petition).

the seller continues to hold legal title to the property, while the buyer is said to have a "beneficial interest." Yet it is the buyer who is in possession and who is liable for taxes and other charges on the property. In fact, the seller's interest is more like that of a secured party than like that of an owner.

In some cases from other states, the courts have held that the seller in a land sale contract may or must sign the petition as owner; in others, the buyer may or must sign it.[14] Those that call for the buyer to sign, however, are preferable. Because the buyer is in possession and pays taxes, he or she is the party most affected by an annexation. Once final payment is made—a matter over which the seller has no control—the buyer will succeed to legal title. In those circumstances, it is apparent that the buyer's interest is more important than the seller's and that the buyer is the more appropriate party to sign. If a city attempted to annex a parcel subject to a land sale contract with only the signature of the seller, a court might very reasonably determine that the petition was inadequate because the effective owner of the property had not signed.

[e] Holder of a timber deed

Under North Carolina common law, a timber deed conveys to the grantee a fee simple interest in the timber on the land in question. Once the timber is cut, the interest terminates automatically. There is currently some uncertainty about whether the provisions of the Uniform Commercial Code have modified the common law in a way that converts interests in timber deeds from real property into personal property.[15]

---

14. *E.g.,* City of Phoenix v. State *ex rel.* Harless, 137 P.2d 783 (Ariz. 1943) (annexation petition; buyers under land sale contract are owners); Town of Sheridan v. Nesbitt, 227 P.2d 1000 (Colo. 1950) (disconnection petition; buyer under land sale contract is owner); Petition of Brandt, 62 N.W.2d 816 (Minn. 1954) (petition to establish drainage district; court holds that a seller under a land sale contract is not the owner); State v. City of Rochester, 109 N.W.2d 44 (Minn. 1961) (annexation petition; buyer under a land sale contract is owner); *contra,* Hull v. Sangamon River Drainage Dist., 76 N.E. 701 (Ill. 1906) (petition to establish drainage district; court holds that the seller is still the owner as long as the deed remains in escrow); City of Cedar Rapids v. Cox, 93 N.W.2d 216 (Iowa 1958) (annexation proceeding; buyer under a land sale contract is not owner of property); Long v. City of Monroe, 251 N.W. 582 (Mich. 1933) (special assessment petition; court holds that buyer under land sale contract is not the owner).

15. *See* Fordham v. Eason, 351 N.C. 151, 521 S.E.2d 701 (1999) and the discussion on this point in DAVID M. LAWRENCE, LOCAL GOVERNMENT PROPERTY TRANSACTIONS IN NORTH CAROLINA § 611B (Institute of Government, 2d edition, 2000).

But even if such deeds continue to convey a fee simple interest in the timber, their holders should not be considered property owners for purposes of signing an annexation petition. Their interest is temporary and relates only to materials—the timber—that will shortly be removed from the land altogether. While no cases dealing specifically with timber deeds have been found, a few cases dealing with other extractive interests support the conclusion that such holders need not sign an annexation petition.[16]

Section 4.04. Who May Sign a Petition As (or on Behalf of) an Owner?

[a] Introduction

The fee simple interest in property can be owned by an individual, a number of individuals, a variety of artificial persons (e.g., corporations or partnerships), someone acting on behalf of another, or a combination of the above. If the property is owned by a single individual, obviously that person (or a person acting as his or her authorized agent or attorney) must sign the petition. This section considers who may or must sign when the owner is, or includes, two or more individuals, an artificial entity, or a person acting on behalf of someone else, such as a trustee.

As discussed at length in the first volume of this series, it is difficult to challenge a voluntary annexation in court.[17] As a practical matter, such a challenge can come only from an owner of the property being annexed or from another city seeking to annex the same property. If no other city is seeking to annex the property, and if no owner objects to the annexation, the failure of all owners to sign the annexation petition is irrelevant as a practical matter. Those who did not sign are assumed to acquiesce in the annexation.[18]

16. *In re* Annexation of Approximately 280 Acres, 615 N.E.2d 43 (Ill. Ct. App. 1993) (annexation petition need not be signed by owners of mineral interests even though courts have characterized such interests as fee interests in the mineral estate). *But see* Enyeart v. Board of Supervisors, 427 P.2d 509 (Cal. 1967) (anti-incorporation petition may be signed by holders of oil and gas leases, which are freehold interests in California. Such leases are normally for much longer periods than timber deeds, however).

17. Standing to challenge an annexation is discussed in Volume 1, chapter 7.

18. In Davis v. City of Archdale, 61 N.C. App. 393, 301 S.E.2d 129 (1983), persons who owned property near an annexation area challenged the annexation on the ground that not all spouses signed the petition for property held by the entireties. The city

[b] Multiple owners

If property is owned by more than one person or entity, each is an owner and each must sign the petition. The most common form of joint ownership is property owned by a married couple. They hold title as *tenants by the entireties*, and each must sign any deed conveying the property. Because both own the property, both must sign any petition for annexing it.[19] Of course, if one spouse appoints the other as agent to sign on behalf of both, only that one signature is needed.[20]

If property is owned by two or more persons who are not married, they are *tenants in common*. In this case, too, each must sign the petition seeking annexation of the property,[21] although one tenant in common may authorize another tenant to sign on his or her behalf.[22]

To annex a condominium complex, a city must obtain the signatures of the owners of every unit in the complex. The board of directors of the condominium owners' association may not sign on behalf of owners of individual units.

[c] Life tenants or remaindermen

A *life estate* is an estate in land limited in duration by the length of a specific person's life—most commonly, the person in possession, the *life tenant*. Once the person whose life measures the estate dies, title passes to the *remainderman* or the *reversioner*. If title passes (or reverts) to the person who created the life estate, that person is the reversioner; if it passes to a third person, that person is the remainderman. The issue for this section is who should sign an annexation petition for property held in a life estate—the life tenant, the remainderman or reversioner, or both?

---

admitted the truth of that allegation, but the court held that the plaintiffs were without standing to bring the suit. None of the nonsigning owners challenged the annexation.

19. *E.g.,* Long v. City of Monroe, 251 N.W. 582 (Mich. 1933) (special assessment petition; signature of husband alone insufficient).

20. *E.g.,* McCune v. City of Phoenix, 317 P.2d 537 (Ariz. 1957) (wife signed for property owned by husband, and both testified that he had authorized her to do so; held, signature was adequate).

21. *E.g.,* Ahern v. Board of Improvement Dist. No. 3, 61 S.W. 575 (Ark. 1901) (special assessment petition); Merritt v. City of Kewanee, 51 N.E. 867 (Ill. 1898) (special assessment petition); *In re* Territory of Riveredge Twp., 545 N.E.2d 1287 (Ohio. Ct. App. 1988) (annexation petition).

22. Powers v. City of Cordele, 238 S.E.2d 721 (Ga. Ct. App. 1977) (one owner may sign annexation petition for self and as agent for other owners).

All the cases dealing with life estates and petitions are quite old, and examples can be found of cases giving each of the three possible answers to this question.[23] The better rule, however, appears to be that both the life tenant and the remainderman (or reversioner) must sign, as suggested in a very old case from Maryland involving paving assessments.

> It is true that, in the absence, as in our state, of any special legislation on the subject, the life-tenant must pay all the ordinary annual taxes levied on the property, and also keep down the interest on encumbrances out of the rents and profits. But, in case of an assessment for a betterment on real estate, the rule would seem to be different. Such betterment is regarded as an encumbrance to which the tenant for life must contribute to the extent of the interest during his life on the money paid, and at his death the remainder-man must bear the charge of the principal. . . . And are there not good reasons why he should be thus excluded? The theory upon which such assessments are thrown upon the property owners, and not upon the public generally, is that their property is specially enhanced in value by such improvements. Now, a life-tenancy is of very uncertain duration, and probably in most cases the reversioner would reap much the larger part of the benefits to be derived from the improvement, and this makes it eminently proper that he should be united with the life-tenant in the application.[24]

[d] Artificial persons

Corporations. If a corporation is small or locally based, it is often possible to obtain the signature of the corporation's president on an annexation petition, but it is not necessary to do so. If the petition is signed by an officer with apparent authority to do so, it is valid unless

---

23. *E.g.,* People *ex rel.* Guthrie v. Barnes, 62 N.E. 207 (Ill. 1901) (life tenant was owner for purpose of petition to establish drainage district); *In re* Incorporation of Mountville Borough, 31 Pa. Super. 18 (1906) (life tenant is proper signatory for incorporation petition); Ahern v. Board of Improvement Dist. No. 3, 61 S.W. 575 (Ark. 1901) (remainderman is proper signatory of special assessment petition); Warren v. Lower Salt Creek Drainage Dist., 147 N.E. 248 (Ill. 1925) (both life tenant and remainderman should sign petition to abolish drainage district).

24. Mayor, etc. of City of Baltimore v. Boyd, 20 A. 1028, 1029 (Md. 1885).

the corporation itself protests. The earliest cases often required a corporation's board of directors to formally authorize a corporate officer to sign an annexation or other sort of petition.[25] More recent cases have taken a more forgiving stance. The modern rule is that if a petition is signed by a proper corporate officer, it will be presumed that the officer was acting within his or her authority and that the signature is valid unless there is specific evidence to the contrary.[26]

National corporations often file powers of attorney in the office of the local register of deeds, granting one or more local company officials the authority to sign documents and take other actions on behalf of the corporation. Such a power of attorney normally is sufficient to authorize officials to sign annexation petitions on behalf of the corporation.[27]

Government bodies. If property is owned by another local government entity, the governing body of that entity should authorize the signing of the petition and designate someone to sign it on its behalf.[28]

Partnerships. Section 59-39 of the General Statutes provides that each partner of a partnership may bind the partnership in matters of partnership business, unless that partner has in fact no authority to bind the partnership and the other party to the transaction knows the partner has no authority. In a limited partnership, only the general partner (or partners) has this power to bind the partnership.[29]

25. *E.g.,* Kahn v. Board of Supervisors, 21 P. 849 (Cal. 1889) (president and secretary may not bind corporation by signing street-paving assessment petition without express authority from board of directors); Morse v. City of Omaha, 93 N.W. 7344 (Neb. 1903) (corporation's president may not sign special assessment petition and thereby bind corporation without special authorization from board of directors).

26. *E.g.,* Gorman v. City of Phoenix, 258 P.2d 424 (Ariz. 1953) (plant manager may sign for General Motors, and there is no requirement that board of directors authorize signature); Kalamazoo Twp. v. Stamm, 64 N.W.2d 595 (Mich. 1954) (court upholds officer's signature on annexation petition on behalf of corporation in absence of any evidence that officer did not have authority to sign.); Appeal of Braddock Twp., 24 A.2d 705 (Pa. Super. Ct. 1942) (court will presume that corporation's vice president was acting within authority in signing annexation petition).

27. The statutory short form power of attorney, set out in G.S. 32A-1, includes the authority to manage property and therefore probably includes authority to sign annexation petitions. G.S. 132A-2(1).

28. *See* Mueller v. City of Milwaukee, 37 N.W.2d 464 (Wis. 1949) (county's property was properly included in annexation after county commissioners adopted resolution authorizing county officials to sign on behalf of county). N.C. Gen. Stat. § 153A-12 provides that county powers are to be exercised by board of county commissioners or at its direction.

29. G.S. 59-403(a).

Therefore, in the normal case, partnership property may be included in an annexation if any partner—or, in a limited partnership, any general partner—signs the petition.[30]

Churches. As religious bodies hold property in a variety of ways, a city receiving a petition for annexation of a church or other property owned by a religious entity should begin by ascertaining in what or whose name the property is held. The case law indicates that it is best to have the governing board or official of the owning entity authorize signing the petition and direct who may sign on behalf of the owning entity.[31]

[e] Those holding property on behalf of another

Trusts. If property is held in a trust, the trustee (not the beneficiary) holds legal title to the property. As holder of the legal title, the trustee seems the appropriate party to sign a petition to annex trust property, and the cases from other states support that conclusion.[32] Furthermore, G.S. 36A-136 indicates that a trustee has general control over trust property, which reinforces the conclusion that the trustee should sign any annexation petition.

Executors and administrators. Under G.S. 28A-15-2, title to real property left by a decedent is vested either in that person's heirs or, if there is a will, in that person's devisees. The heirs or devisees are the owners of the property and should therefore sign any annexation petition regarding the property. As the executor or administrator of the

---

30. This statutory system accords with North Carolina case law and case law from other states, which hold that a partner may sign a petition on behalf of the partnership and thereby bind it. *E.g.,* Brown v. Town of Hillsboro, 185 N.C. 368, 117 S.E. 41 (1923) (partner may sign special assessment petition for partnership); City of Malvern v. Nunn, 192 S.W. 909 (Ark. 1917) (partner may sign special assessment petition for partnership).

31. City of Elizabethtown v. Purcell, 293 S.W. 1096 (Ky. 1927) (there must be some kind of authority from church authorities to actual signer of special assessment petition); State v. Mayor, etc. of Borough of Fairview, 43 A. 578 (N.J. 1899) (special assessment petition signed by "Trustees of the Church of the Sacred Heart, per W. A. Purcell, Treas." valid when church minutes show express authorization from board to treasurer to sign); Allen v. City of Portland, 58 P. 509 (Oreg. 1899) (church clerk validly signed special assessment petition upon resolution by vestrymen).

32. *E.g.,* Crocher v. Abel, 180 N.E. 852 (Ill. 1932) (holding that bank holding property as trustee under a will was proper party to sign an annexation petition); Portsmouth Sav. Bank v. City of Omaha, 93 N.W. 231 (Neb. 1903) (will made decedent's wife and son "trustees and executors" of several lots, under a trust lasting for the remainder of the wife's life; the court held that the trust was owner of the property and the trustees were the proper parties to sign a special assessment petition).

estate is not the owner, his or her signature is not adequate to annex property in the estate.[33]

Guardians. Under G.S. 35A-1251 and 35A-1252, guardians appointed for incompetents and minors have general charge of their wards' property. The statutes make it clear that the ward is owner of the property but give the guardian broad authority to manage it. Under G.S. 35A-1301, the guardian must secure the approval of the clerk of court to sell or mortgage the property, but those are more significant acts than agreeing to annexation of the property. Thus, it appears that if a property owner is a minor or an incompetent, the annexation petition should be signed by the owner's guardian.[34]

[f] Agents and representatives

Whether agents can sign petitions was tested in the 1923 case of *Brown v. Town of Hillsboro*.[35] Among the grounds put forward by the plaintiff in this broad-based challenge to a special assessment project was the claim that one signature on the special assessment petition was invalid, because it was not the signature of the property owners. The signer testified that he had acted as agent for the owners for many years and had transacted all their business involving the property. Furthermore, the owners had not objected to his signing the petition. On the basis of that testimony, the trial court held that the signature was valid, and the supreme court affirmed. The opinion does not reveal whether the signer had indicated on the petition that he was agent for the owners or had simply signed it with his own name.

It is clear from *Brown* that an agent, representative, or attorney may sign an annexation petition on behalf of an owner. The courts of some states require the fact of the agency to be made clear on the face of the petition,[36] but others do not and hold that agents' signatures are valid

33. This conclusion is consistent with the national case law. *See, e.g.,* City of Phoenix v. State *ex rel.* Harless, 137 P.2d 783 (Ariz. 1943) (administrator of estate may not sign petition because not owner); Ahern v. Board of Improvement Dist. No. 3, 61 S.W. 575 (Ark. 1901) (executor may not sign special assessment petition even if has power of sale, because not owner of property); Kahn v. Board of Supervisors, 21 P. 849 (Cal. 1889) (executors and administrators may not sign special assessment petition).

34. *See* City of Malvern v. Nunn, 192 S.W. 909 (Ark. 1917) (guardian may sign special assessment petition on behalf of minors and other persons under a disability).

35. 185 N.C. 368, 117 S.E. 41 (1923).

36. *E.g.,* Merritt v. City of Kewanee, 51 N.E. 867 (Ill. 1898) (person signing special assessment petition as agent should say so in petition); Twp of South Middleton v.

unless the owner protests.[37] Given the silence of the *Brown* opinion about how the agent signed the petition, it is more likely that he did not indicate his agency on the petition and that, therefore, North Carolina would join the states that do not require such an explicit acknowledgment of the agency. That outcome does make sense: if the owner disagrees with the annexation, there is ample opportunity to make that fact known and to repudiate the alleged agent's signature. (It would still be good practice, however, for agents to identify themselves as such when signing petitions, and some cities require them to do so.) Furthermore, the cases generally permit the agent to sign, even if his or her authority to do so was oral rather than written,[38] and *Brown* is consistent with that rule.

Section 4.05. Changes in the Petition

[a] Introduction

Once a city receives an annexation petition, a number of events might change the petition or the names of persons who are or should be signatories of the petition. An owner might decide to oppose the annexation and seek to remove his or her signature from the petition. Another owner might decide to join the petition. An owner who signed the petition might later sell the property to someone else. Property owners might wish to submit a more accurate description of the property or include a better map of the annexation area. This section addresses the effect these changes have on the validity of the petition.

[b] Withdrawal of property

Right of withdrawal. The North Carolina supreme court has held that a property owner may withdraw his or her property from the petition at any time up to the point the city council adopts the annexation ordi-

---

Borough of Carlisle, 346 A.2d 869 (Pa. Cmmw. Ct. 1975) (agent may sign annexation petition if agency is disclosed in petition itself).

37. *E.g.,* McCune v. City of Phoenix, 317 P.2d 537 (Ariz. 1957); City of Columbus v. Sohl, 8 N.E. 299 (Ohio 1886).

38. *E.g.,* McCune v. City of Phoenix, 317 P.2d 537 (Ariz. 1957); Merritt v. City of Kewanee, 51 N.E. 867 (Ill. 1898); Twp of South Middleton v. Borough of Carlisle, 346 A.2d 869 (Pa. Cmmw. Ct. 1975).

nance. By doing so, the owner not only bars annexation of his or her own property but also invalidates the entire petition.

The supreme court reached these conclusions in the 1979 case of *Allman v. City of Newton*.[39] While engaged in a race with Conover to annex a set of properties lying between the two cities, Newton received a petition from a group of property owners seeking voluntary annexation. At the public hearing on the petition, four persons who had signed the petition submitted written requests that their names and properties be removed from the petition; at a continued session of the hearing, two other persons made the same request. The city denied the property owners' requests to withdraw their signatures and proceeded, over their protests, to annex their properties (along with the properties of owners who had not sought to withdraw). When these property owners brought suit to challenge the annexation, the trial court held that they were entitled to withdraw and that Newton's annexation ordinance was invalid because of their withdrawal. The supreme court affirmed.

The supreme court relied on the 1941 case of *Idol v. Hanes*,[40] which held that persons who had signed a petition to form a sanitary district could withdraw their signatures at any time before final action was taken on the petition. The court emphasized that voluntary annexation is based on the freely given consent of the property owners and held, therefore, that petitioners had the right "to reconsider their initial decision and withdraw from the petition at any time before final action thereupon."[41] Because the final action on an annexation petition is adoption of the annexation ordinance, signers of a petition may withdraw their properties from the annexation at any time before the ordinance is adopted.[42]

Effect of withdrawal. If a property owner does withdraw his or her property, that action invalidates the entire petition and makes it impossible for the city to annex any of the property included in the original petition. In *Allman*, the city argued that if the court upheld the petitioners' right to withdraw their signatures, the city should then be allowed to annex the properties whose owners continued to request annexation. The court, however, disagreed. It pointed out that G.S. 160A-31 permits a city to annex "the territory described in the petition"—unlike the two

39. 297 N.C. 506, 256 S.E.2d 216 (1979).
40. 219 N.C. 723, 14 S.E.2d 801 (1941).
41. *Allman*, 297 N.C. at 517, 256 S.E.2d at 223.
42. *Id.* at 518, 256 S.E.2d at 224.

involuntary annexation statutes, which permit a city to annex all or a part of the territory described in the resolution of intent and the notice of public hearing.

> If the General Assembly had intended to authorize cities proceed-
> ing pursuant to a petition for voluntary annexation to annex
> merely a part of the area described in the petition, it would have
> so provided as it has explicitly done in [the involuntary statutes].
> The absence of such statutory authorization, in light of the
> explicit provisions for it in the involuntary annexation statutes, is
> cogent evidence that the General Assembly intended a petition for
> voluntary annexation to stand or fall as a unity.[43]

Thus, if a signer of a voluntary annexation petition withdraws his or her signature from the petition before the city adopts the annexation ordinance, the city should ask any remaining owners to present a new petition and begin the process anew.

[c] Addition of signatories and/or properties

The *Allman* case focuses on how *withdrawing* properties affects the petition. What about changes in the other direction—*adding* signatories or properties to an existing petition? Are such changes permissible, or do they also invalidate the original petition and necessitate filing a new one?

Adding properties. Given the logic of the *Allman* court, an attempt to add properties to the petition appears to invalidate the original petition. The court in *Allman* emphasized that the voluntary annexation statute permits a city council to annex "the territory described in the petition." After the withdrawal of property, the territory before the council was different from that described in the petition; therefore the council could not adopt an annexation ordinance. The same would be true if property were added to the petition—the territory before the council would be different from that described in the petition; therefore the council could not adopt an annexation ordinance.

A city might counter that the council was in fact annexing the territory described in the *amended* version of the petition. That is, the

43. *Id.* at 519, 256 S.E.2d at 225-26. The court was discussing the voluntary contiguous annexation statute, G.S. 160A-31 (d), but the voluntary satellite annexation statute, G.S. 160A-58.2, contains identical language.

city might argue that the council is entitled to annex the territory described in the petition as that petition stands just before the council acts, rather than only as it was described in the original petition. According to this argument, the territory described in the original petition would be susceptible to amendment during the time the proposal is before the council, and the council would be entitled to annex whatever territory was described at the time the council acted. That territory, after all, would still be "the territory described in the petition." The difficulty with this argument, of course, is that it could equally well be applied to changes that withdraw property from the petition: they too would modify the original description of territory, and the council would be acting with respect to the most recent version of the description. But the supreme court would not allow the city of Newton to annex a territorial area modified in that way. Rather, it appears to have read the statute's language as referring only to the territory described in the original petition. There's no logical way to read that language one way when property is added and another when it is removed. Therefore, the conclusion remains that the statute does not allow adding property to a petition once that petition has been presented to the city council.

Adding signatories but not properties. The *Allman* case does not speak as strongly to what occurs when persons wish to add signatures, but not new properties, to a petition. For example, a wife might have signed for property held by the entireties, and her husband might wish to come in later and sign the petition as well. The "territory described in the petition" has not changed, and therefore the statutory basis for the *Allman* holding is not present. Furthermore, there are good policy reasons for permitting such additional signatures. As noted above in Section 4.04[f], one person can sign a petition as the agent of another without proving that agency by any written document. When one does sign as agent, however, particularly under an oral agency, there remain issues related to whether there was in fact an agency and therefore whether the petition is sufficient. Those issues can be resolved if the principal later signs the petition directly. If such a person did not authorize the alleged agency, he or she may challenge the validity of the annexation; by not challenging the annexation, such a person essentially admits that the agency existed. That being the case, there is no harm in allowing the person to also demonstrate agreement with the annexation by signing the petition after it has been submitted to the city.

There is one situation, however, in which adding a signature to a petition later might not be permitted. If the city is in an annexation dispute with another city and seeks to show that it has prior jurisdiction to conduct its annexation, the absence of an owner's signature at the time the petition was received by the city would probably be fatal to its chances of achieving prior jurisdiction to annex at that time.[44] Adding the signature at a later date would not revive the city's claim to prior jurisdiction.

Changes in ownership. If a parcel of property included in an annexation petition is sold after the petition is presented to the city council but before the council adopts the annexation ordinance, the logic of *Allman* suggests that the petition is no longer adequate.[45] It no longer contains the signatures of the owners of the property being annexed, and the new owners clearly could challenge the validity of any attempted annexation. If the new owners wish the annexation to go forward, however, there seems to be no reason not to allow them to substitute their signatures for those of the previous owners. There has been no change in the property seeking annexation, and therefore the statutory basis of the *Allman* holding is inapplicable. For the same reasons that it seems permissible to allow additional owners to sign the petition after its presentation to the city council—as long as no property is added—it seems permissible to allow new owners to substitute their signatures for those of the previous owners.

In addition, because the previous owner signed the petition when it was presented to the council and because that person presumably owned the property at that time, such a petition is not subject to a challenge of the city's prior jurisdiction to proceed with the annexation. The petition was valid when presented and thus gave the city prior jurisdiction.

[d] Changes to the map or description of the annexation area

The voluntary contiguous annexation statute, G.S. 160A-31(b), requires that the petition include a description of the territory proposed for

44. Volume I, section 3.03[b] in the text at note 23 suggests that the lack of an owner's signature would mean that the city had not taken a valid first step in its annexation and therefore that prior jurisdiction would not accrue.

45. If the property is sold after the ordinance is adopted but before its effective date, the conveyance has no effect on the validity of the annexation; the property still becomes part of the city on the effective date.

annexation. The voluntary satellite annexation statute, G.S. 160A-58.1(c), requires that the petition include a metes and bounds description of the territory proposed for annexation, as well as a map showing the relationship of the annexation area to the city (and to other, nearby, cities). (These property description and map requirements are described more fully in the next section.) An annexation description might contain minor errors or be otherwise inadequate, or the map might have been omitted. Usually there seems to be no harm in allowing the petitioners to correct the error and amend the petition by presenting a corrected description or map before the council acts, making it unnecessary to require a new petition and a new beginning of the process. Of course, in a race with another city to annex the same territory, a petition with an inaccurate boundary description or an inadequate map (or no map at all) could be considered insufficient to give the city prior jurisdiction.[46] In such a situation, the city might need to begin the process anew with a fresh and correct petition.

Section 4.06. Form of the Petition

[a] Required content

The voluntary contiguous annexation statute requires that the petition include the signature and address of each owner of property in the proposed annexation area, while the satellite statute requires that it contain the name, address, and signature of each owner. In addition, both petitions must describe the proposed annexation area. The satellite statute requires that the petition include a metes and bounds description of the area. (*See* section 6.01 of Volume 1 of this series, where the meaning of a *metes and bounds* description is fully discussed.) The contiguous annexation statute, on the other hand, does not specify the form of the description, which suggests that something

46. *But see* In re Annexation Ordinance of Conover, 297 N.C. 506, 256 S.E.2d 216 (1979), in which the court held that petitioners challenging an involuntary annexation had suffered no material injury from the fact that the metes and bounds description in the city's resolution of intent omitted one small parcel. A comparable error in the petition's description of a voluntary annexation area might also be found immaterial and not affect whether the petition gives the city prior jurisdiction. The complete failure to include a map in a satellite petition, however, is more serious and would likely lead to a loss of prior jurisdiction. The need for a valid first step in an annexation to achieve prior jurisdiction is discussed at length in Volume 1, section 3.03[b] of this series.

less than a metes and bounds description will satisfy the statute. Perhaps, for example, a reference to a subdivision plat—"lots 2, 3, and 4 of the Angelic Acres subdivision, located on Mason Highway, and recorded in Plat Book 18, page 47"—would suffice. What is necessary is a description that makes clear what property is being included in the proposed annexation and makes it possible to locate it on the ground.

Despite the statute's flexibility, many cities require persons seeking voluntary contiguous annexation to include a metes and bounds description, or even a surveyed description, in their contiguous annexation petition. Other cities require petitioners to include copies of the deeds for their properties, on the assumption that the deeds contain adequate boundary descriptions. Most cities want a metes and bounds description of the property for the annexation ordinance (even though the statute does not require that the ordinance include such a description), and it makes sense to have the petitioner, rather than the city, provide it.

The satellite annexation statute (but not the contiguous statute) also requires that petitioners include a map showing the proposed annexation area and its relationship to the city. (In addition, if there is a substantial question as to whether the annexation is closer to a city other than to the annexing city, the map must also show the area's relation to that other city.) Some cities require that persons seeking contiguous annexation also submit such a map.

In addition, some cities require petitioners to provide information that will assist it in meeting its obligations to rural fire departments and private solid waste collectors.[47] For example, the city might require each petitioner to state his or her property's Parcel Identification Number and its assessed value or to indicate whether the property owner has a contract with a private solid waste collector.

If the city is in a county subject to Section 5 of the federal Voting Rights Act and the area proposed for annexation includes properties in residential use, the city will need to know the race of current residents. That information will have to be submitted to the U.S. Department of Justice as part of the process of preclearing the annexation. (See Volume 1, section 13.01 for a list of covered counties and a description of the effect of that statute on annexations.) The easiest way to obtain that information is to require it from petitioners as a condition of accepting the annexation petition.

---

47. These obligations are detailed in Volume 1, chapters 9 and 10 of this series.

[b] Vested rights

General Statutes 153A-344.1 and 160A-385.1 establish one of the ways in which development rights may become vested: through local government approval of a site-specific development plan or a phased development plan. (Section 8.02[b] of Volume 1 of this series discusses the concept of vested development rights under county or city land-use regulations.) The two voluntary annexation statutes permit a city to adopt an ordinance requiring property owners petitioning for annexation to submit a signed statement as to whether vested development rights gained pursuant to either of these two statutes are associated with their property.[48] If the statement claims such rights, the city may require the property owners to prove that fact. More important, if the owners declare that there are no such rights, the city may rely on that assertion. The statutes provide that property owners are bound by these statements, which terminate any such vested development rights as might in fact have existed.

It should be noted that the vested rights statement permitted by the annexation statutes is limited to vested rights gained pursuant to G.S. 153A-344.1 or 160A-385.1. If a property is subject to development rights that have vested in other ways (as described in section 8.02[b] of Volume 1), those rights will continue after annexation—unless the property owner relinquishes them—regardless of whether they are disclosed in any signed statement included with the annexation petition.

Section 4.07. Fees

A number of cities require persons seeking voluntary annexation to submit a fee along with their petition in order to meet some or all of the city's costs in processing the annexation and ensuring that the petition is in proper order. The voluntary annexation statutes are silent as to the propriety of imposing fees on petitioners, but the principles enunciated by the North Carolina supreme court in *Homebuilders Association of*

---

48. The model annexation petitions set out in the North Carolina League of Municipalities' (NCLM) handbooks include a vested rights statement. Before including such a statement in its petition, a city should be sure it has adopted an ordinance requiring the statement. (MECHANICS OF ANNEXATION UNDER 5,000 POPULATION and MECHANICS OF ANNEXATION 5,000 OR MORE POPULATION, are available from NCLM, PO Box 3069, Raleigh, NC 27602, or through its Web site, http://nclm.org/Publications/pubs.pdf (last visited September 23, 2003).

Charlotte, Inc. v. City of Charlotte appear to give adequate support for such fees.[49]

At issue in *Homebuilders* were a variety of fees charged by the city as a condition of issuing various permits or other regulatory permissions or as part of the rezoning process. The statutes that authorized the city to enact the various regulations said nothing about charging fees to those being regulated, but the supreme court held that the statutes implicitly permitted such fees. Some of the fees under review involved rezoning requests or special-use permit requests, both of which involve legislative action on the part of the city. Therefore, the decision allows a city to impose a fee to cover its costs whenever it undertakes legislative actions having particular relevance to specific persons. As an annexation is also a legislative action that obviously has special relevance to owners of annexed property, the case supports charging annexation petitioners a fee to recover the city's costs in processing the annexation proposal.

Section 4.08. Annexing Property Owned by the City

Both of the voluntary annexation statutes make special provision for annexing property owned by the annexing city.[50] Even though the city is the owner, the property must meet the same standards as privately owned property: that is, it must be contiguous for a contiguous annexation or meet the several standards established for satellite annexations. But instead of presenting a petition to itself, the city council initiates the annexation process by adopting a resolution of intent. This resolution must state the city's intent to annex the property, describe it, and set a date for a public hearing. In addition, if the city is proceeding under the contiguous annexation statute, the resolution must affirm that the property is in fact contiguous to the existing city limits.[51]

Once the city council adopts this resolution of intent, it follows the same procedure for annexing city-owned property as it does for privately owned property.

49. 336 N.C. 37, 442 S.E.2d 45 (1994).

50. G.S. 160A-31(g) for contiguous property and G.S. 160A-58.7 for satellite property.

51. The annexation handbooks of NCLM contain forms for the necessary resolutions.

The Annexation Process

The Annexation Process

Section 5.01. Overview of the Process

The statutory procedure for a voluntary annexation, which is essentially the same for both contiguous and satellite annexations, may be briefly summarized as follows:

1. Property owners present a petition to the city, asking for annexation.
2. The city clerk investigates the sufficiency of the petition and certifies its sufficiency to the city council.[1]
3. The city council calls a public hearing on the proposed annexation.
4. At the hearing, the public comments upon the sufficiency of the petition and the desirability of the annexation.
5. After the public hearing, the council adopts an ordinance annexing the property included in the petition.

The remainder of this chapter fleshes out this summary.

Section 5.02. The Statutory Steps

[a] Submission of the petition

A voluntary annexation formally begins when property owners present a petition seeking annexation to the city council.[2] Some city councils have rules of procedure governing the presentation of petitions, rules that owners need to check out and follow. As noted in earlier chapters, the statutes require that the petition describe the property for which

---

1. The determinations involved in establishing sufficiency are explained below in section 5.02(b).

2. N.C. Gen. Stat. § 160A-31(a) and (b) (hereinafter G.S.) for contiguous annexations, and G.S. 160A-58.1(a) and (c) for satellite annexations.

annexation is sought and include the signature and address of each owner of real property in the proposed annexation area.[3] The satellite annexation statute also requires that the petition include (1) the printed name and signature of each owner and (2) a map that shows the proposed annexation area and its relationship to the annexing city. If there is a substantial question as to whether the proposed satellite area is closer to another city—and is therefore ineligible for satellite annexation—the map must also show the proposed annexation area's relationship to that other city.[4]

G.S. 160A-31(b) of the contiguous annexation statute sets out a model form for the petition, which can also serve as a model for a satellite annexation statute. The annexation handbooks published by the North Carolina League of Municipalities (NCLM) also contain forms for these petitions.[5]

[b] The clerk's investigation

Once the city council receives the petition, it should determine whether it is interested in annexing the proposed area, or at least in investigating the question. If the council is not interested in annexing the proposed area under any circumstances, there is no point in continuing the process; the council should simply table the petition and move on to other business.

Assuming that the council is interested in pursuing or investigating the annexation, the council then refers the petition to the city clerk, who investigates the petition's sufficiency.[6] That task involves the following investigations:

1. Ascertaining that the petition adequately describes the property(ies) for which annexation is sought. Although the

---

3. As discussed in section 4.02, a satellite annexation petition need not include the signatures of owners of property that is wholly exempt from taxation or of the following kinds of owners: railroad companies, public utilities, or electric or telephone membership corporations.

4. Section 4.06[a] suggests a number of other items that a city might, at its own discretion, require in any voluntary annexation petition.

5. NCLM, MECHANICS OF ANNEXATION (UNDER 5,000 POPULATION and 5,000 OR MORE POPULATION), available from NCLM, PO Box 3069, Raleigh, NC 27602, or through its Web site: http://www.nclm.org/Publications/pubs.pdf (last visited September 23, 2003).

6. G.S. 160A-31(c) for contiguous annexations, and G.S. 160A-58.2 for satellite annexations. The NCLM annexation handbooks include a model form of a resolution directing the clerk to investigate the petition's sufficiency.

contiguous statute contains no standards for this description, the clerk must at least determine that it is possible to locate the property on the ground. In the case of the satellite statute, however, the clerk must verify that the petition includes a metes and bounds description and is accompanied by a map showing the proposed annexation area and its relationship to the annexing city and, if necessary, any other nearby city or cities.

2. Establishing the ownership of the real property included in the proposed annexation area. It is not necessary, in the usual case, to undertake a title search for each included property. Rather, the clerk may use the property tax records to determine the owners, then use the grantor index in the register of deeds' office to verify that the owners listed there have not recently conveyed the property to someone else. In difficult cases, the city clerk should seek the assistance of the city attorney.

3. Ensuring that each owner so determined has signed the petition and that the petition includes each owner's address. In addition, in a satellite annexation, the petition must include each owner's printed name.

4. *In a contiguous annexation*, making certain that the proposed annexation area is in fact currently contiguous to the existing city limits.

5. *In a satellite annexation*, verifying that the proposed annexation area meets the five statutory standards for satellite annexation.[7]

6. *In all voluntary annexations*, determining that any other information the city itself requires is included in the annexation petition.

Once the clerk has completed this investigation, he or she "certifies the results" of the investigation to the city council.[8]

Each of the statutes seems to assume that the city council and staff will have had no prior knowledge or notice of the annexation proposal before it is submitted to the council. In many cities, however, the property owners present the petition to the clerk or some other city official well before a council meeting and the clerk investigates the

---

7. These standards are the subject of chapter 3.
8. The NCLM annexation handbooks include a model form for the clerk's certificate.

petition's sufficiency before the matter ever comes before the council. If a city follows such a procedure, the council can receive the petition and the clerk's certificate at the same meeting and move immediately to the next step in the process.

[c] The public hearing

Once the clerk certifies the petition as sufficient, the council may schedule a public hearing on the proposed annexation.[9] Once the council sets the date, the clerk must publish notice of the hearing in a newspaper that circulates generally within the annexing city.[10] This notice must be published once, at least ten days before the date of the public hearing, in accordance with Rule 6 of the North Carolina Rules of Civil Procedure.[11] That rule specifies that in computing time periods, the day of publication is not counted, but the last day of the required time period is counted unless the last day is a Saturday, Sunday, or holiday; in that case, the time period ends at the end of the next day that is not a holiday. Thus, if a hearing will be held on October 22, the latest the notice may be published is October 12. The ten-day period in this instance starts with October 13 and ends on October 22. Neither voluntary annexation statute specifies the particulars of the published notice. At a minimum, it should give the date, time, location, and purpose of the public hearing and include a map or description of the annexation area clear enough to permit readers to recognize the property involved. The NCLM annexation handbooks mentioned above contain models for this notice.

The two voluntary annexation statutes include slightly different provisions governing who may speak at the public hearing and what they might speak about:

In a *contiguous annexation*, the statute calls for hearing from (1) any owner of property in the annexation area who alleges that the petition contains an error (e.g., "I didn't sign this petition") and (2) any resident of the city who questions the necessity for the annexation.

---

9. G.S. 160A-31(c) and (d) for contiguous annexations, and G.S. 160A-58.2 for satellite annexations.

10. The contiguous statute provides for a posted notice if there is no newspaper of general circulation within the annexing city. There is no comparable provision in the satellite statute, apparently on the assumption—pretty safe—that there is no city or town in North Carolina within which there is no newspaper of general circulation.

11. G.S. 1A-1, Rule 6.

In a *satellite annexation*, the statute calls for hearing from (1) any resident of the annexation area, (2) any owner of property within the annexation area, and (3) any resident of the annexing city. All such persons may speak both to the sufficiency of the petition and the desirability of the proposed annexation.

As a practical matter, a city council will usually allow comment on the proposed annexation from any person who wishes to speak.

[d] Board action

Once the public hearing is concluded, the city council may act on the petition. It may do so immediately after the hearing, or it may wait until a subsequent meeting. The statute does not establish a deadline for council action; therefore, if the council does not act immediately, the matter probably remains before the council unless and until the petitioner withdraws the petition or some other city actively seeks to annex some or all of the property included in the petition.[12]

If the council decides to annex the property described in the petition, it must make certain findings specified in the annexation statutes. The *contiguous* annexation statute requires that the council find that the "petition meets the requirements" of the statute.[13] The *satellite* annexation statute is more specific but probably not, in its effect, appreciably different. In a satellite annexation, the council must find that

- the area meets the five standards of satellite annexations;
- all necessary owners have signed the petition;
- the petition is otherwise valid; and
- annexation would best serve the public health, safety, and welfare of city citizens and inhabitants of the annexation area.

Normally, a council includes these findings in the annexation ordinance itself. The model ordinances set out in the annexation handbooks of the NCLM include examples of these findings.

If the council is able to make the required findings, it may adopt an ordinance that annexes the property described in the petition. As

12. Section 3.04 of Volume 1 of this series discusses the ways in which the courts might find that an annexation proceeding has been abandoned when another city is attempting to annex the same property.

13. G.S. 160A-31(d).

discussed in section 4.05, the statute requires that the ordinance annex precisely the property included in the annexation petition as originally presented to the city council. If the council is not willing to annex the entire proposed annexation area, it should reject the petition and ask the property owners to submit a new one including only the property the city is willing to annex.

The council may make the ordinance effective immediately upon adoption or at any date within six months of the day the ordinance is adopted.

6

City Services and Regulations after Annexation

6

City Services and Regulations after Annexation

Section 6.01. The General Rule

Section 160A-58.3 of the North Carolina General Statutes (hereinafter G.S.), part of the satellite annexation statute, provides that "from and after the effective date of the annexation ordinance, the annexed area and its citizens and property are subject to all debts, laws, ordinances and regulations of the annexing city, and are entitled to the same privileges and benefits as other parts of the city." The contiguous annexation statute, G.S. 160A-31(e), says the same thing in almost identical language. In general, this means that the city must provide the citizens and property of the annexation area with the same package of services it provides citizens and property within the existing city. In addition, citizens and property within the annexation area become subject to the ordinances and other regulations currently in effect within the existing city. If the annexation area is not currently subject to city zoning, the city has up to sixty days from the effective date of annexation to extend zoning regulations to the annexation area, at which time any county zoning ceases to be effective. (The impact of annexation on zoning is described more fully in section 8.02[b] of Volume 1.) The involuntary annexation statutes include special provisions for properties within an annexation area that are subject to use-value taxation. Because neither of the voluntary annexation statutes contain comparable provisions, properties in a voluntary annexation subject to use-value taxation are treated no differently than any other property so annexed.[1]

For most city services, the service requirements are straightforward. The city must immediately extend law enforcement to the annexation area, assume responsibility for street maintenance, provide for solid

---

1. One city, Huntersville, has obtained local legislation that extends the use-value system to voluntary annexations. S.L. 1999-19.

waste collection, and so on.[2] The city's responsibilities for water and sewer services in the annexation area, however, are slightly more nuanced, and the next section examines those two services. In addition, the satellite statute and appellate case law establish some special rules for satellite areas; those rules are discussed in the final section of this chapter.

Section 6.02. Water and Sewer Services

[a] Introduction

Neither voluntary annexation statute makes any special provision for extending water or sewer services to the annexation area. This silence contrasts with the two involuntary annexation statutes, which include several specific provisions about extending those services. It will be useful to look briefly at some of the specific provisions of the involuntary statutes as a way of framing discussion of the city's responsibilities for water and sewer in a voluntary annexation.

1. If a city provides water or sewer services to properties in the existing city, it must provide those services to properties in the involuntary annexation area.
2. The statutes set out specific timetables under which the city must extend major trunk water mains and sewer outfall lines so that distribution and collection lines can then be extended to individual properties in the involuntary annexation area.
3. The statute applicable to cities of five thousand or more population permits owners of annexed property to require the city to extend water or sewer lines to their specific property.
4. If installation of sewer lines is not economically feasible due to the unique topography of the involuntary annexation area, the city may provide septic system maintenance and repair services until it is able to extend sewer service to the area.

---

2. The statements in this sentence assume that the annexing city is already providing these services to its citizens. If a city is not providing a particular service within the existing city, it need not do so in the annexation area.

[b] Responsibility for extending water or sewer lines

Although the involuntary annexation statutes impose an express statutory duty to extend water lines or sewer lines to all properties within the annexation area, the voluntary annexation statutes contain no such express duty. Instead, the city's responsibilities for utility line extension are those imposed by the general laws regulating municipal utility services. Because the statutes regulating city public enterprises set out in Article 16 of G.S. Chapter 160A do not address a city's responsibility for extending such utility services throughout the city, we must look to the common law of public utility operations, which applies to the provision of city utilities within city boundaries.[3] Although there is no developed case law on this subject in North Carolina, cases from the courts of other states present a generally consistent approach to these issues.

The basic rule, articulated in a number of cases, is that public authorities have discretion in determining whether, and where, to extend water and sewer lines within a city. There is no absolute duty to extend utility lines to every property in the city simply because it is within the city. Three cases illustrate this rule.

An early case is *Lawrence v. Richards*,[4] a 1913 case from Maine. In 1903 the Maine legislature created the Gardiner Water District, with a territory about 6 miles long and about 1.5 miles wide. The district's primary purpose was to purchase an existing private water system that provided service only in the more congested parts of the district—an area about a mile in diameter—and that purpose was carried out. The legislation created a three-member board of trustees to govern the district and required that the district's voters approve all bonds necessary to finance capital improvements in excess of $10,000. The plaintiff, who lived at some distance from the water system but within the district, demanded that the district extend lines to his property. The cost would have been $45,000; the trustees refused, and the plaintiff brought suit to force the extension. The plaintiff's position was that the district trustees had no discretion in this matter but were under a duty to extend district lines to all properties in the district. The Maine court disagreed, saying the following:

---

3. *E.g.,* Dale v. City of Morganton, 270 N.C. 567, 155 S.E.2d 136 (1967); Fulghum v. Town of Selma, 238 N.C. 100, 76 S.E.2d 368 (1953).

4. 88 A. 92 (Me. 1913).

If [the plaintiff's] contention has real merit, the consequence is
that the trustees, acting for the district, are legally bound to
supply water to all inhabitants, no matter how large the cost of
the undertaking, now [*sic*] how small the revenue, no matter
how ruinous and destructive the result might be to the financial
ability of the district to carry on its operations. That this contention is not sound is, we think, easily demonstrable. The area of
the district [in which plaintiff lives] is scatteringly settled. The
elevation in some places is considerably higher than the system's
reservoir. It does not need the testimony of expert engineers to
satisfy a reasoning mind that under such conditions the expense
necessarily to be incurred in performing the duty, as it is claimed
to be, of supplying every inhabitant of the district with water
would practically be destructive of the purposes of the charter. It
would create a burden too heavy to be borne.

. . .

We think then that the contention that as a matter of law every
individual in the district has the right to have the water brought to
him cannot be sustained. But if the district is not in law bound to
supply all, who is to determine to what extent the system shall be
expanded, and who shall thereby be supplied? The power to do
this must necessarily be vested in the trustees.[5]

A comparable case is *City of Greenwood v. Provine*,[6] decided by the
Mississippi supreme court in 1926. The city's original water system
served all its residents when built, but the system had not been extended
to all the properties in a subsequent annexation area. The plaintiff
owned a house in that annexation area, some two city blocks (700 feet)
from the nearest water line, and he brought an action to require the city
to extend a line to his house. He argued that he was entitled to the water
line simply because his property was now within the city. The Mississippi
court disagreed, making the following comments:

Certainly it is not the law that a resident of a municipality, living
in a remote corner thereof, may compel the city authorities to
extend its water mains to his premises regardless of the cost and
expense to the city, merely because the citizen resides within the

5. *Id.* at 95.
6. 108 So. 284 (Miss. 1926).

boundaries of the municipality. The extension of the water system from one part of the city where already laid to another part depends upon the reasonableness of such extension, considering the demand for it, the number of water subscribers, and the revenue to be obtained from furnishing the water.[7]

A final illustration is *Rose v. Plymouth Town*,[8] decided in Utah in 1946. The defendant, a very small municipality, had been incorporated a few years earlier for the sole purpose of obtaining a federal loan and constructing a water system. After incorporation, the town's voters approved two bond issues, the town obtained the loan, and the town constructed the water system. The system was connected to every home within the town except the plaintiff's. He therefore brought suit to force the town to extend the lines to his home as well. The court's opinion makes it clear how small this town was and what construction of a line to the plaintiff's home would mean. The town's annual revenues were less than $150 and were limited by Utah law to less than $200. Since incorporation, the plaintiff had paid almost $200 in taxes to the town, so it appears that his property was among the town's most valuable. On these facts, the Utah court, using language very much like that used by the Maine court more than thirty years earlier, held that the town was not under any duty to extend the lines; rather, whether to extend the lines was a matter within the discretion of the town officials.[9]

Although no North Carolina cases are directly in point, two cases do suggest that the North Carolina courts would agree with this national body of law. In the 1941 case of *Town of Dunn v. Tew*,[10] the town was seeking to enforce a tax lien against the defendants' property, which had been annexed several years before. The defendants made two arguments against their liability for the tax: (1) there had been no voter approval of the annexation (which had been accomplished by act of the General Assembly); and (2) the town had not extended town services to their property. The court dealt at considerable length with the first

7. *Id.* at 286.

8. 173 P.2d 285 (Utah 1946).

9. Other cases that reach comparable conclusions include Browne v. City of Bentonville, 126 S.W. 93 (Ark. 1910); Marr v. City of Glendale, 181 P. 671 (Cal. Ct. App. 1919); Levitt v. Public Utilities Comm'n, 159 A. 878 (Conn. 1932); Moore v. City Council of Harrodsburg, 105 S.W. 926 (Ky. 1907); and State *ex rel.* Cox v. City of Raymore, 723 S.W.2d 910 (Mo. Ct. App. 1987).

10. 219 N.C. 286, 13 S.E.2d 536 (1941).

issue, holding that voter approval was not necessary. On the second issue, the court simply said that these "other matters complained of by defendants as to improvements in the section, were in the sound discretion of plaintiff, the municipality."[11] In the 1957 case of *Ramsey v. Rollins*,[12] the plaintiff sought to stop the county from issuing bonds to construct a water distribution system that would serve some, but not all, parts of the county. The plaintiff argued that using tax money to support such a system deprived citizens of the unserved portions of the county of both due process and equal protection. The court rejected both arguments, citing cases from other states that upheld counties' ability to levy taxes throughout the county and use the tax proceeds to provide utility services to only a portion of the county.

The out-of-state cases discussed above and other comparable cases set out the following sorts of considerations that a city may legitimately rely upon in deciding whether to extend water or sewer services to a particular property within the city's boundaries:

- The cost of making the extension,[13]
- The prospective revenues from the extension,[14]
- Whether there are current customers along the extended line,[15]
- Prospective growth along the extended line,[16]
- The city's supply of water,[17] and
- Whether the property owner will pay the cost of extension.[18]

It is clear, then, that a city may have a policy that requires owners of property at some specified distance from existing utility lines to pay the cost of extending those lines to their property.[19] And, if a city has such a policy, it may certainly enforce that policy within a voluntary annexation

---

11. *Id.* at 286, 13 S.E.2d at 540.

12. 246 N.C. 647, 100 S.E.2d 55 (1957).

13. Lukrawka v. Spring Valley Water Co., 146 P. 640 (Cal. 1915); Lawrence v. Richards, 88 A. 92 (Me. 1913).

14. *Id.*

15. Reid Development Corp. v. Parsippany-Troy Hills Township, 107 A.2d 20 (N.J. Super. Ct. App. Div. 1954).

16. Marr v. City of Glendale, 181 P. 671 (Cal. Ct. App. 1919).

17. Lukrawka v. Spring Valley Water Co., 146 P. 640 (Cal. 1915).

18. Rose v. Plymouth Town, 173 P.2d 285 (Utah 1946).

19. *E.g.,* Wolff v. Louisville Water Co., 302 S.W.2d 104 (Ky. 1957); State *ex rel.* Kennedy v. Public Service Comm'n, 42 S.W.2d 349 (Mo. 1931).

area. But it may also be that if a property owner is willing to pay the cost, the city is under a duty to make the extension.[20]

Because there is no absolute duty to extend water or sewer lines to any property that has been voluntarily annexed, there is obviously no statutory timetable under which such extensions must be made.

[c] City extension policies

A city that has properties in the city that are not served by the water or sewer systems, or that plans to voluntarily annex property without extending utility lines to the property, would be well-advised to adopt policies that set out the circumstances under which it will extend utility lines and the financial responsibilities for such extensions. (Such policies are also necessary when a city undertakes an involuntary annexation.) If the city has such policies and has followed them, a property owner interested in petitioning the city for annexation will know what those policies are and can plan accordingly. Furthermore, a city that has adopted and followed such policies—rather than extending or not extending utilities through a set of random, ad hoc decisions—is much better able to defend itself against a charge that its extension decisions are based on illegitimate considerations.

It appears that such policies might permit the city to provide septic tank cleanout services to property owners in lieu of extending sewer service, at least if the cost of extending sewer lines is extraordinary. The involuntary annexation statutes expressly permit such a policy,[21] but these express statutory provisions declare rather than create the law. Cities receive their authority to engage in public enterprises, including wastewater systems, from G.S. Chapter 160A, Article 16; G.S. 160A-311, which is part of that article, defines wastewater systems to include "septic tank systems or other on-site collection or disposal facilities or systems." Furthermore, before the involuntary annexation statutes were amended to make specific reference to septic tank cleanout services, the North Carolina supreme court had held, in *Greene v. Town of Valdese*, that plans to offer such services in lieu of extending sewer lines to certain below-grade properties satisfied a town's responsibilities under the involuntary annexation statute.[22] Importantly, the court also

---

20. *See* Rose v. Plymouth Town, 173 P.2d 285 (Utah 1946).
21. G.S. 160A-35(3)b and 160A-47(3)b.
22. *Valdese*, 306 N.C. 79, 291 S.E.2d 630 (1982).

noted that the town had had a policy in place calling for septic tank cleanout whenever sewer line extension was extraordinarily expensive and had followed that policy within the existing town.

Section 6.03. Special Rules for Satellite Areas

[a] Statutory rules

The satellite annexation statute includes two sections that create special rules for financing public enterprise services in a satellite area and limit the city's regulatory powers immediately outside a satellite area.

Enterprise services. Normally a city is under a statutory duty to apply a common rate structure for its public enterprises to all customers within the city; that is, the city must apply the same rate structure to all residential customers, or to all commercial customers, and so on. The satellite annexation statute, however, permits a city to establish a different, higher rate structure for its satellite areas than that established for properties within the primary city limits.[23] The statute is somewhat ambiguous in this matter, but it appears that a city with two or more satellite areas is only allowed to have a single class of rates for satellite properties; it may not, that is, establish a separate rate structure for each satellite area.

The opening sentence of the statute permitting such a special class of enterprise rates is phrased permissively—the city *may* establish special rates for enterprise services to satellite properties. The closing sentence of the section, however, carries the possibility of an apparent mandate. That sentence directs a city providing enterprise services to satellite areas to review annually its costs (other than debt service) for doing so and to "take such steps as may be necessary" to ensure that the operating costs of providing the services do not exceed the revenues received from satellite customers of the services. (This direction apparently applies even when a city subsidizes an enterprise service with general fund revenues.) If the necessary cost accounting demonstrates that the current rate structure applied to satellite areas does not recoup the costs of providing an enterprise's services to those areas, the statute seems to require the city to raise rates within satellite areas in order to do so.

---

23. G.S. 160A-58.5.

Extraterritorial regulatory powers. G.S. 160A-360 entitles cities to an extraterritorial jurisdiction for land-use regulation, most commonly the area within one mile of the city's corporate limits. In addition, G.S. 160A-193 permits a city to summarily abate public health nuisances within the city and within one mile of the city's corporate limits. G.S. 160A-58.4, part of the satellite annexation statute, states that these extraterritorial regulatory authorizations do not apply to satellite areas. That is, a city may exercise extraterritorial land-use powers or abate public health nuisances extraterritorially only within areas measured from the city's primary limits. Annexation of satellite areas does not expand the extraterritorial regulatory jurisdiction of a city.

[b] Spot zoning

The North Carolina supreme court has defined *spot zoning* as a zoning ordinance or amendment that

> singles out and reclassifies a relatively small tract owned by a single person and surrounded by a much larger area uniformly zoned, so as to impose upon the small tract greater restrictions than those imposed upon the larger area, or so as to relieve the small tract from restrictions to which the rest of the area is subjected.[24]

In 2002 the court decided *Good Neighbors of South Davidson v. Town of Denton*, a case that illustrates the unique susceptibility of satellite areas to a charge of spot zoning.[25] In 1978 a chemical company purchased a fifty-acre tract in Davidson County; sometime before 1990, it placed a chemical storage facility on the tract. In 1990 the county commenced zoning of the area and zoned the tract and the surrounding community as rural agricultural. Thus, the chemical storage area became a nonconforming use. In 1991, and again in 1994, the chemical company unsuccessfully petitioned the county to rezone the tract to a manufacturing use so as to permit either expansion of the existing facility or commencement of manufacturing at the site. In 1998 the company petitioned the town of Denton for satellite annexation of the tract, and the town did so. A few weeks later, the town council

24. Blades v. City of Raleigh, 280 N.C. 531, 549, 187 S.E.2d 35, 45 (1972).
25. 355 N.C. 254, 559 S.E.2d 768 (2002).

rezoned ten acres of the tract to light industrial and forty acres to heavy industrial, and the neighbors brought suit to challenge the rezoning. The supreme court held that the new zoning was spot zoning, even though the surrounding properties were zoned by a different jurisdiction, the county. Spot zoning is not per se illegal; the zoning jurisdiction may defend the zoning by showing a reasonable basis for its actions. The court in *Good Neighbors,* however, rejected the town's attempts to justify the spot zoning, even accusing the town of a "cavalier unreasonableness" in its actions.[26] It invalidated the zoning change.

The consequence of this decision is that a city that begins zoning in a satellite area surrounded by properties still subject to county zoning jurisdiction will have to pay some attention to the county's zoning of those surrounding properties. This is particularly true if the annexation is motivated by the property owner's wish to escape county regulation; in that case, the city will have to show a reasonable basis for any spot zoning that results from its assumption of zoning authority.

26. *Id.* at 262, 559 S.E.2d at 774.

Appendix A

Major North Carolina Statutes
Discussed in the Text or Footnotes

General Statute (G.S.) Section	Page
160A-31(a)	4-10–20, 5-3–4
160A-31(b)	4-25–26, 5-3–4
160A-31(c)	5-4–7
160A-31(d)	5-6–8
160A-31(e)	6-3–10
160A-31(f)	ch. 2, passim
160A-31(g)	4-28
160A-31(h)	4-27
160A-36(b)	2-12–14
160A-58.1(a)	4-3–20, 5-3–4
160A-58.1(b)	ch. 3, passim
160A-58.1(b2)	3-7
160A-58.1(c)	4-25–26,5-3–4
160A-58.1(d)	4-27
160A-58.2	5-4–8
160A-58.3	6-3–10
160A-58.4	6-11
160A-58.5	6-10
160A-58.7	3-5, 4-28

Appendix B

North Carolina Appellate Cases Discussed or Cited in the Text or Footnotes

If a case is *discussed* in the text or a footnote, its page number is set in **boldface** type. If the case is only *cited* in a footnote, the page number is set in regular roman type.

Case	Page
Allman v. City of Newton	**4-9n, 4-21–24**
Amick v. Town of Stallings	**2-12–14**
Blades v. City of Raleigh	6-11n
Brown v. Town of Hillsboro	**4-18n, 4-19–20**
City of Burlington v. Town of Elon College	**3-9**
City of Kannapolis v. City of Concord	**2-5–6**
Conover v. Newton	**3-10**, 4-25n
County of Brunswick v. Town of Bolivia	**4-8–9**
Dale v. City of Morganton	6-5n
Davis v. City of Archdale	**4-14n**
Fordham v. Eason	4-13n
Fulghum v. Town of Selma	6-5n
Good Neighbors of South Davidson v. Town of Denton	**6-11–12**
Greene v. Town of Valdese	6-9n

Case	Page
Hawks v. Town of Valdese	**2-3–5**, 3-4
Homebuilders Association of Charlotte, Inc. v. City of Charlotte	**4-27–28**
Idol v. Hanes	4-21
Joyner v. Town of Weaverville	**3-9, 3-13n, 3-14n**
Ramsey v. Rollins	**6-8**
Three Guys Real Estate v. Harnett County	3-12n
Town of Dunn v. Tew	**6-7–8**
Town of Seven Devils v. Town of Sugar Mountain	2-14n
Town of Valdese v. Burke, Inc.	**2-18–19**
Whiting Manufacturing Co. v. Carolina Aluminum Co.	2-21n
Williamson v. Avant	**3-12–13**

Appendix C

The North Carolina Voluntary Annexation Statutes

Contiguous Annexations

§ 160A-31. Annexation by petition.

(a) The governing board of any municipality may annex by ordinance any area contiguous to its boundaries upon presentation to the governing board of a petition signed by the owners of all the real property located within such area. The petition shall be signed by each owner of real property in the area and shall contain the address of each such owner.

(b) The petition shall be prepared in substantially the following form:

DATE:

To the _____ (name of governing board) of the (City or Town) of _____

1. We the undersigned owners of real property respectfully request that the area described in paragraph 2 below be annexed to the (City or Town) of_____

2. The area to be annexed is contiguous to the (City or Town) of _____ and the boundaries of such territory are as follows:

(c) Upon receipt of the petition, the municipal governing board shall cause the clerk of the municipality to investigate the sufficiency thereof and to certify the result of his investigation. Upon receipt of the certification, the municipal governing board shall fix a date for a public hearing on the question of annexation, and shall cause notice of the public hearing to be published once in a newspaper having general circulation in the municipality at least 10 days prior to the date of the public hearing; provided, if there be no such paper, the governing board shall have notices posted in three or more public places within the area to be annexed and three or more public places within the municipality.

(d) At the public hearing all persons owning property in the area to be annexed who allege an error in the petition shall be given an opportunity to be heard, as well as residents of the municipality who question the necessity for annexation. The governing board shall then determine whether the petition meets the requirements of this section. Upon a finding that the petition meets the requirements of this section, the governing board shall have authority to pass an ordinance annexing the territory described in the petition. The governing board shall have authority to make the annexing ordinance effective immediately or on any specified date within six months from the date of passage of the ordinance.

(e) From and after the effective date of the annexation ordinance, the territory and its citizens and property shall be subject to all debts, laws, ordinances and regulations in force in such municipality and shall be entitled to the same privileges and benefits as other parts of such municipality. Real and personal property in the newly annexed territory on the January 1 immediately preceding the beginning of the fiscal year in which the annexation becomes effective is subject to municipal taxes as provided in G.S. 160A-58.10. If the effective date of annexation falls between June 1 and June 30, and the effective date of the privilege license tax ordinance of the annexing municipality is June 1, then businesses in the area to be annexed shall be liable for taxes imposed in such ordinance from and after the effective date of annexation.

(f) For purposes of this section, an area shall be deemed "contiguous" if, at the time the petition is submitted, such area either abuts directly on the municipal boundary or is separated from the municipal boundary by a street or street right-of-way, a creek or river, or the right-of-way of a railroad or other public service corporation, lands owned by the municipality or some other political subdivision, or lands owned by the State of North Carolina. In describing the area to be annexed in the annexation ordinance, the municipal governing board may include within the description any territory described in this subsection which separates the municipal boundary from the area petitioning for annexation.

(g) The governing board may initiate annexation of contiguous property owned by the municipality by adopting a resolution stating its intent to annex the property, in lieu of filing a petition. The resolution shall contain an adequate description of the property, state that the property is contiguous to the municipal boundaries and fix a date for a public hearing on the question of annexation. Notice of the public hearing shall be published as provided in subsection (c) of this section. The governing board may hold the public hearing and adopt the annexation ordinance as provided in subsection (d) of this section.

(h) A city council which receives a petition for annexation under this section may by ordinance require that the petitioners file a signed statement declaring whether or not vested rights with respect to the properties subject to the petition have been established under G.S. 160A-385.1 or G.S. 153A-344.1. If the statement declares that such rights have been established, the city may require petitioners to provide proof of such rights. A statement which declares that no vested rights have been established under G.S. 160A-385.1 or G.S. 153A-344.1 shall be binding on the landowner and any such vested right shall be terminated. (1947, c. 725, s. 8; 1959, c. 713; 1973, c. 426, s. 74; 1975, c. 576, s. 2; 1977, c. 517, s. 4; 1987, c. 562, s. 1; 1989 (Reg. Sess., 1990), c. 996, s. 3.)

§ 160A-31.1. Assumption of debt.

(a) If the city has annexed under this Part any area which is served by a rural fire department and which is in:
  (1) An insurance district defined under G.S. 153A-233;
  (2) A rural fire protection district under Article 3A of Chapter 69 of the General Statutes; or
  (3) A fire service district under Article 16 of Chapter 153A of the General Statutes,
then beginning with the effective date of annexation the city shall pay annually a proportionate share of any payments due on any debt (including principal and interest) relating to facilities or equipment of the rural fire department, if the debt was existing at the time of submission of the petition for annexation to the city under this Part. The rural fire department shall make available to the city not later than 30 days following a written request from the city, information concerning such debt. The rural fire department forfeits its rights under this section if it fails to make a good faith response within 45 days following receipt of the written request for information from the city, provided that the city's written request so states by specific reference to this section.

(b) The annual payments from the city to the rural fire department on such shared debt service shall be calculated as follows:

(1) The rural fire department shall certify to the city each year the amount that will be expended for debt service subject to be shared by the city as provided by subsection (a) of this section; and

(2) The amount determined under subdivision (1) of this subsection shall be multiplied by the percentage determined by dividing the assessed valuation of the area of the district annexed by the assessed valuation of the entire district, each such valuation to be fixed as of the date the annexation ordinance becomes effective.

(c) This section does not apply in any year as to any annexed area(s) for which the payment calculated under this section as to all annexation ordinances adopted under this Part by a city during a particular calendar year does not exceed one hundred dollars ($100.00).

(d) The city and rural fire department shall jointly present a payment schedule to the Local Government Commission for approval and no payment may be made until such schedule is approved. The Local Government Commission shall approve a payment schedule agreed upon between the city and the rural fire department in cases where the assessed valuation of the district may not readily be determined, if there is a reasonable basis for the agreement. (1989, c. 598, s. 2.)

Satellite Annexations

Part 4. Annexation of Noncontiguous Areas.

§ 160A-58. Definitions.

The words and phrases defined in this section have the meanings indicated when used in this Part unless the context clearly requires another meaning:

(1) "City" means any city, town, or village without regard to population, except cities not qualified to receive gasoline tax allocations under G.S. 136-41.2.

(2) "Primary corporate limits" means the corporate limits of a city as defined in its charter, enlarged or diminished by subsequent annexations or exclusions of contiguous territory pursuant to Parts 1, 2, and 3 of this Article or local acts of the General Assembly.

(3) "Satellite corporate limits" means the corporate limits of a noncontiguous area annexed pursuant to this Part or a local act authorizing or effecting noncontiguous annexations. (1973, c. 1173, s. 2.)

§ 160A-58.1. Petition for annexation; standards.

(a) Upon receipt of a valid petition signed by all of the owners of real property in the area described therein, a city may annex an area not contiguous to its primary corporate limits when the area meets the standards set out in subsection (b) of this section. The petition need not be signed by the owners of real property that is wholly exempt from property taxation under the Constitution and laws of North Carolina, nor by railroad companies, public utilities as defined in G.S. 62-3(23), or electric or telephone membership corporations.

(b) A noncontiguous area proposed for annexation must meet all of the following standards:

(1) The nearest point on the proposed satellite corporate limits must be not more than three miles from the primary corporate limits of the annexing city.

(2) No point on the proposed satellite corporate limits may be closer to the primary corporate limits of another city than to the primary corporate limits of the annexing city, except as set forth in subsection (b2) of this section.

(3) The area must be so situated that the annexing city will be able to provide the same services within the proposed satellite corporate limits that it provides within its primary corporate limits.

(4) If the area proposed for annexation, or any portion thereof, is a subdivision as defined in G.S. 160A-376, all of the subdivision must be included.

(5) The area within the proposed satellite corporate limits, when added to the area within all other satellite corporate limits, may not exceed ten percent (10%) of the area within the primary corporate limits of the annexing city. This subdivision does not apply to the Cities of Claremont, Concord, Conover, Newton, Sanford, Salisbury, and Southport, and the Towns of Catawba, Maiden, Midland, Swansboro, and Warsaw.

(b1) A noncontiguous area proposed for annexation must meet all of the following standards:

(1) The nearest point on the proposed satellite corporate limits must be not more than three miles from the primary corporate limits of the annexing city.

(2) No point on the proposed satellite corporate limits may be closer to the primary corporate limits of another city than to the primary corporate limits of the annexing city, except as set forth in subsection (b2) of this section.

(3) The area must be so situated that the annexing city will be able to provide the same services within the proposed satellite corporate limits that it provides within its primary corporate limits.

(4) If the area proposed for annexation, or any portion thereof, is a subdivision as defined in G.S. 160A-376, all of the subdivision must be included.

(5) Repealed by Session Laws 2001-37, s. 1, effective April 26, 2001.

This subsection applies to the Cities of Marion, Oxford, and Rockingham and the Towns of Calabash, Catawba, Dallas, Godwin, Louisburg, Mocksville, Pembroke, Rutherfordton, and Waynesville only.

(b2) A city may annex a noncontiguous area that does not meet the standard set out in subdivision (b)(2) of this section if the city has entered into an annexation agreement pursuant to Part 6 of this Article with the city to which a point on the proposed satellite corporate limits is closer and the agreement states that the other city will not annex the area but does not say that the annexing city will not annex the area. The annexing city shall comply with all other requirements of this section.

(c) The petition shall contain the names, addresses, and signatures of all owners of real property within the proposed satellite corporate limits (except owners not required to sign by subsection (a)), shall describe the area proposed for annexation by metes and bounds, and shall have attached thereto a map showing the area proposed for annexation with relation to the primary corporate limits of the annexing city. When there is any substantial question as to whether the area may be closer to another city than to the annexing city, the map shall also show the area proposed for annexation with relation to the primary corporate limits of the other city. The city council may prescribe the form of the petition.

(d) A city council which receives a petition for annexation under this section may by ordinance require that the petitioners file a signed statement declaring whether or not vested rights with respect to the properties subject to the petition have been established under G.S. 160A-385.1 or G.S. 153A-344.1. If the statement declares that such rights have been established, the city may require petitioners to provide proof of such rights. A statement which declares that no vested rights have been established under G.S. 160A-385.1 or G.S. 153A-344.1 shall be binding on the landowner and any such vested rights shall be terminated. (1973, c. 1173, s. 2; 1989 (Reg. Sess., 1990), c. 996, s. 4; 1997-2, s. 1; 2001-37, s. 1; 2001-72, s. 1; 2001-438, s. 1; 2002-121, s. 1.)

§ 160A-58.2. Public hearing.

Upon receipt of a petition for annexation under this Part, the city council shall cause the city clerk to investigate the petition, and to certify the results of his investigation. If the clerk certifies that upon investigation the petition appears to be valid, the council shall fix a date for a public hearing on the annexation. Notice of the hearing shall be published once at least 10 days before the date of hearing.

At the hearing, any person residing in or owning property in the area proposed for annexation and any resident of the annexing city may appear and be heard on the questions of the sufficiency of the petition and the desirability of the annexation. If the council then finds and determines that (i) the area described in the petition meets all of the standards set out in G.S. 160A-58.1(b), (ii) the petition bears the signatures of all of the owners of real property within the area proposed for annexation (except those not required to sign by G.S. 160A-58.1(a)), (iii) the petition is otherwise valid, and (iv) the public health, safety and welfare of the inhabitants of the city and of the area proposed for annexation will be best served by the annexation, the council may adopt an ordinance annexing the area described in the petition. The ordinance may be made effective immediately or on any specified date within six months from the date of passage. (1973, c. 1173, s. 2.)

§ 160A-58.2A. Assumption of debt.

(a) If the city has annexed under this Part any area which is served by a rural fire department and which is in:

    (1) An insurance district defined under G.S. 153A-233;

    (2) A rural fire protection district under Article 3A of Chapter 69 of the General Statutes; or

    (3) A fire service district under Article 16 of Chapter 153A of the General Statutes,

then beginning with the effective date of annexation the city shall pay annually a proportionate share of any payments due on any debt (including principal and interest) relating to facilities or equipment of the rural fire department, if the debt was existing at the time of submission of the petition for annexation to the city under this Part. The rural fire department shall make available to the city not later than 30 days following a written request from the city, information concerning such debt. The rural fire department forfeits its rights under this section if it fails to make a good faith response within 45 days following receipt of the written request for information from the city, provided that the city's written request so states by specific reference to this section.

(b) The annual payments from the city to the rural fire department on such shared debt service shall be calculated as follows:

    (1) The rural fire department shall certify to the city each year the amount that will be expended for debt service subject to be shared by the city as provided by subsection (a) of this section; and

    (2) The amount determined under subdivision (1) of this subsection shall be multiplied by the percentage determined by dividing the assessed valuation of the area of the district annexed by the assessed valuation of the entire district, each such valuation to be fixed as of the date the annexation ordinance becomes effective.

(c) This section does not apply in any year as to any annexed area(s) for which the payment calculated under this section as to all annexation ordinances adopted under this Part by a city during a particular calendar year does not exceed one hundred dollars ($100.00).

(d) The city and rural fire department shall jointly present a payment schedule to the Local Government Commission for approval and no payment may be made until such schedule is approved. The Local

Government Commission shall approve a payment schedule agreed upon between the city and the rural fire department in cases where the assessed valuation of the district may not readily be determined, if there is a reasonable basis for the agreement. (1989, c. 598, s. 3.)

§ 160A-58.3. Annexed area subject to city taxes and debts.

From and after the effective date of the annexation ordinance, the annexed area and its citizens and property are subject to all debts, laws, ordinances and regulations of the annexing city, and are entitled to the same privileges and benefits as other parts of the city. Real and personal property in the newly annexed territory on the January 1 immediately preceding the beginning of the fiscal year in which the annexation becomes effective is subject to municipal taxes as provided in G.S. 160A-58.10. If the effective date of annexation falls between June 1 and June 30, and the privilege licenses of the annexing city are due on June 1, then businesses in the annexed area are liable for privilege license taxes at the full-year rate. (1973, c. 1173, s. 2; 1975, c. 576, s. 5; 1977, c. 517, s. 7.)

§ 160A-58.4. Extraterritorial powers.

Satellite corporate limits shall not be considered a part of the city's corporate limits for the purposes of extraterritorial land-use regulation pursuant to G.S. 160A-360, or abatement of public health nuisances pursuant to G.S. 160A-193. However, a city's power to regulate land use pursuant to Chapter 160A, Article 19, or to abate public health nuisances pursuant to G.S. 160A-193, shall be the same within satellite corporate limits as within its primary corporate limits. (1973, c. 1173, s. 2.)

§ 160A-58.5. Special rates for water, sewer and other enterprises.

For the purposes of G.S. 160A-314, provision of public enterprise services within satellite corporate limits shall be considered provision of service for special classes of service distinct from the classes of service provided within the primary corporate limits of the city, and the city may fix and enforce schedules of rents, rates, fees, charges and penalties in excess of those fixed and enforced within the primary corporate limits. A city providing enterprise services within satellite corporate limits shall annually review the cost thereof, and shall take such steps as may be necessary to insure that the current operating costs of such services, excluding debt service on bonds issued to finance services within satellite corporate limits, does not exceed revenues realized therefrom. (1973, c. 1173, s. 2.)

§ 160A-58.6. Transition from satellite to primary corporate limits.

An area annexed pursuant to this Part ceases to constitute satellite corporate limits and becomes a part of the primary corporate limits of a city when, through annexation of intervening territory, the two boundaries touch. (1973, c. 1173, s. 2.)

§ 160A-58.7 Annexation of municipal property.

The city council may initiate annexation of property not contiguous to the primary corporate limits and owned by the city by adopting a resolution stating its intent to annex the property, in lieu of filing a petition. The property must satisfy the requirements of G.S. 160A-58.1. The resolution shall contain an adequate description of the property and fix a date for a public hearing on the question of annexation. Notice of the public hearing shall be published once at least 10 days before the date of the hearing. At the hearing, any resident of the city may appear and be heard on the question of the desirability of the annexation. If the council finds that annexation is in the public interest, it may adopt an ordinance annexing the property. The ordinance may be made effective immediately or on any specified date within six months from the date of passage. (1987, c. 562, s. 2.)

§ 160A-58.8. Recording and Reporting.

Annexations made under this part shall be recorded and reported in the same manner as under G.S. 160A-29. (1987, c. 879, s. 4.)

Index

www.ingramcontent.com/pod-product-compliance
Lightning Source LLC
Chambersburg PA
CBHW061831220326
41599CB00027B/5255